What I Wish
My Christian Friends Knew
about Judaism

What I Wish My Christian Friends Knew about Judaism

ROBERT SCHOEN

LOYOLA PRESS.
A JESUIT MINISTRY
Chicago

LOYOLA PRESS.
A JESUIT MINISTRY

3441 N. Ashland Avenue
Chicago, Illinois 60657
(800) 621-1008
www.loyolapress.com

Author photo: Ben Ailes

Cover design by Adam Moroschan
Interior design by Megan Duffy Rostan

Library of Congress Cataloging-in-Publication Data
Schoen, Robert.
    What I wish my Christian friends knew about Judaism / Robert Schoen.
        p. cm.
Includes bibliographical references.
    ISBN-13: 978-0-8294-1777-7
    ISBN-10: 0-8294-1777-X
    1. Judaism. I. Title.
BM562.S45 2004
296'.02'427—dc22

2003024404

Printed in the United States of America
        14 Versa 10 9

To the memory of my grandparents, who crossed an ocean, passed through Ellis Island, and learned a new language so that my parents, their children, and their children's children could live in a land of religious freedom and tolerance.

Contents

Holidays and Festivals

Jewish Life Cycle Events

Home Life, Jewish Beliefs, and Other Interesting Matters

Judaism in the World

Acknowledgments

In the several years I spent putting this book together, I leaned on many people. I was without shame in asking friends, relatives, patients, and virtual strangers to review the manuscript.

A number of people, upon hearing I was writing a book about Judaism, asked to "read" it. I wouldn't let them "read" it unless they agreed to seriously "critique" it. Some declined, but many accepted the challenge. Not one person who reviewed the manuscript—whatever his or her educational, religious, or socioeconomic background—failed to provide me with important information, insights, anecdotes, and religious facts and figures.

Some people who reviewed the manuscript concentrated more on editorial corrections. Others spent more energy on biblical, religious, social, or historical concerns. Regardless of the type or size of the contribution, I appreciate the help of everyone and could not have completed this project without their assistance.

Whenever possible, I incorporated the advice and suggestions given to me. But in the end, I accept full responsibility for any and all mistakes, misstatements, and omissions.

Heartfelt thanks go to Will Adams, who offered enthusiastic encouragement even before a word was written and then read every version of the manuscript. Pulitzer Prize-winning author

Michael Chabon pointed me in the right direction, compelling me to concentrate on the purpose of the project. The late Walter Pakter, a scholar and linguist, passed away before this book went to publication. He gave freely of his vast knowledge of biblical, legal, and world history, and I will miss him.

Special appreciation goes to my friend, the writer Alice Camille, who believed in this book and is deserving of my deepest gratitude.

I wish to express my sincere thanks to Linda Adams, Mike and Gretchen Bailey, Bruce Barrett, Nancy Blachman, Bill Bonville, Bob Branstrom, Carolyn D'Andrea, Claire Davidson, Bill Devore, Barbara Feinstein, Eileen Feldman, Pastor Heidi Gamble, Jaye Griffiths, Professor Avishai Henik, Bobbe Klezmer, Anne Power, Burt Rodgers, Marc and Jan Wasserman, Ken Woolfe, and the East Bay Institute for Contemporary Studies. Everyone helped in large and small ways. My apologies to anyone I've neglected to mention.

I was honored to have the following rabbis review portions of the manuscript, provide essential information about Judaism, and offer their support and encouragement: Rabbi Steven A. Chester, Rabbi Eliezer Finkelman, and Rabbi Mark Diamond. Rabbi Harry A. Manhoff provided valuable resources during my research on early Judeo-Christian history and the Jewish roots of Christian worship. Rabbi Andrea Berlin, who officiated at the marriage ceremony of my wife and myself, also reviewed the manuscript and gave generously of her time and knowledge. Cantor Ilene Keys, who also participated at our wedding, and Cantor Jennie Chabon reviewed the section on the role of the cantor. Joshua Boettiger, currently a rabbinical student, provided valuable insight into Reconstructionist Judaism.

I have had the honor to attend church services with many friends and colleagues over the years, and I learned much from both clergy and congregants. Brian Montone, with whom I attended Mass on several occasions, gave valuable commentary on Catholic history and practices.

Edward Ross Dickinson, professor of history at the University of Cincinnati, reviewed the section on the Holocaust and the rise in Nazism.

Tom McGrath, Jim Manney, and Matthew Diener from Loyola Press offered their confidence and valuable advice, as well as help in understanding the Jewish roots of Christian worship. Vinita Wright and Katherine Faydash contributed their excellent editorial help.

My wonderful parents, Pearl and Michael W. Schoen, provided me with all a son could wish for, including a Jewish home. My sister, Eve Schoen Samet, still remains one of the funniest people I've ever met. I am fortunate to be blessed with creative, talented, and hardworking children: Adam and Marna Schoen and Steve and Michael Chabon.

Throughout this project, I have had the love, support, and tolerance of my wife, Sharon Chabon, who, in her own quiet way, makes my world a more peaceful place in which to live.

R.S.

Preface

Kermit the Frog has said that it's not easy being green. Well, it's not easy being anything. Being Jewish presents its own problems, and through the years I have often wished I could explain to my non-Jewish friends, in a simple, nonthreatening manner, what my religion is all about.

From the Sabbath to circumcision, from Hanukkah to the Holocaust, from bar mitzvah to bagel, how do Jewish religion, history, holidays, lifestyles, and culture make Jews different, and why is that difference so distinctive that we carry it from birth to the grave?

So, I present here a compendium of facts, lore, and opinion. I've checked the facts and the lore in a number of sources. The opinions (and humor) are mine. If you disagree with anything written on these pages, it's OK. As a matter of fact, it's part of the Jewish tradition to disagree.

Robert Schoen
Oakland, California

As a father has compassion for his children,

So the Lord has compassion for those who fear Him.

For He knows how we were made;

He remembers that we are dust.

As for mortals, their days are like grass;

They flourish like a flower of the field;

For the wind passes over it, and it is gone, and its place
knows it no more.

But the steadfast love of the Lord is from everlasting to
everlasting on those who fear Him,

And His righteousness to children's children,

To those who keep His covenant and remember to do His
commandments.

The Lord has established His throne in the heavens,

And His kingdom rules over all.

From Psalm 103
A Psalm of David

The Purpose of This Book

I have never met a Christian who was not in some way curious about Judaism, the Jewish people, or some aspect of the Jewish way of life. Even though Christianity evolved from Judaism and Jesus himself was a Jew, during their religious education and upbringing most Christians learn little about Judaism and the Jews. Often what they do learn is based on myth or hearsay and serves only to increase their curiosity (or multiply their misconceptions) about why Jews do what they do and believe what they believe.

I have also discovered that the more a Christian knows about his or her religion, the more curious that person tends to be about Judaism.

Christians have good reason to be curious. After all, Judaism and Christianity come from the same roots. Our religions share many of the same biblical stories, taken from the Hebrew Scriptures (commonly referred to as the Old Testament). Thus, both Christians and Jews feel comfortable telling the age-old stories of Adam and Eve, David and Goliath, Sodom and Gomorrah, Daniel, Noah, Moses, and Joseph. Both Christians and Jews are steeped in this shared heritage. We can rejoice together in the marvelous stories, lessons to be learned, and wit and wisdom. We also can learn important lessons from those early accounts of tragedies, wars, and other situations that revealed the ultimate power of God.

Many Christians wonder why Jews do not believe in Jesus, and why Jewish children and adults do not study the teachings and stories of the New Testament. When a person is growing up Jewish in America, these questions can be very puzzling and difficult to answer.

Through the years, I have wondered about how best to answer questions that my Christian friends asked. Sometimes, I have given simple explanations about how Christian teachings are not part of the Jewish belief system. I've said that Jews have nothing against Jesus, the New Testament, Catholics, Protestants, or any other Christian denomination or sect—or any non-Jewish religion, for that matter. Questions beget more questions, though, and answers are rarely simple.

Many Christians don't realize that Jews, as a group, are unfamiliar with the New Testament and the teachings of Christianity. Why is this? The New Testament is not part of our heritage, not included in our worship services, and not included in our many religious books. Certainly there are Jewish scholars who study Christian texts and writings. In addition, rabbis and Jewish educators learn about Christianity and other religions as part of their formal training.

However, the average Jewish person has not read the New Testament. I am pleased to say that I have. Not long ago, as part of a university course called "The Bible for Students of Literature," I read the New Testament for the first time. How surprised and pleased I was to find the source of so many common sayings, words of wisdom, and stories. I had no idea! Both the Hebrew Scriptures and the New Testament surely provide the "greatest stories ever told."

Being one of the only Jews taking that course, however, also invited a new series of questions from my classmates. These were questions I had heard through the years about why Jewish people believe certain things, why they perform the rituals they do, what is the significance of the Jewish calendar, and what are the origins of many customs and practices.

I can say this: I believe that in the heart of the Jewish people there exists a deep-seated desire to be permitted to pray in our own way, to observe God the way we wish, and to live a life of peace. I would guess that this desire is similar to that of non-Jews as well. You could call this a basic desire for religious tolerance, and Christians certainly understand this, since virtually every religious group in history has sought religious tolerance and the freedom to worship in its own way. In its time, each group has experienced terrible ordeals, but I am most familiar with the history of the Jewish people, a nation that has been enslaved, expelled from numerous countries, and suffered at the hands of those who wished to exterminate it completely, and a nation that continues to endure persecution in its many subtle and overt forms. The story of Judaism and the Jewish way of life is a complicated one.

Besides normal curiosity, many Christians and other non-Jews desire a basic understanding about the Jewish people and their holidays, customs, and history. This desire often arises as a result of marriage and family relationships, friendships at work, social situations, or church activities.

For example, Christians who have married members of my family have questions about the holidays that they now help celebrate even while maintaining their own religious beliefs. To cite another example, my wife and I have participated in interfaith meetings in an attempt to coordinate efforts and rally political support to help improve social and educational services in our city. In addition, while it is common to have Christmas parties in the workplace or in schools, often Jewish holidays such as Rosh Hashanah (the Jewish New Year) and Hanukkah are also celebrated, raising the curiosity of non-Jews present at the occasions.

I am a layman, and I write from the perspective of someone who considers himself an "average Jewish American." Whether you have a Jewish friend, spouse, employer, employee, or coworker, I hope that as a result of reading this book you become more knowledgeable about the issues of what it means to be a Jew, what the basic tenets and philosophy of Judaism are, and what problems contemporary American Jews face in today's society.

So, I have written this book to satisfy curiosity, answer questions, and offer a resource for inquisitive people.

A Range of Jewish Lifestyles, Beliefs, and Behaviors

Even if I have never been a "practicing" or observant Jew, I'm still Jewish.

Whether I attend religious services or speak or read Hebrew, I'm still Jewish. Regardless of whether I have become a bar mitzvah or been married in a Jewish ceremony (or, for that matter, married another Jewish person), I am still considered Jewish. Even if I've never stepped into a synagogue in my life, if I was born a Jew, I'm *still* a Jew. And if I've converted to Judaism, then I am considered as much a Jew as someone who is born a Jew.

I can renounce my Jewish heritage and religion and convert to another faith, in which case I might consider myself something else. I may even seek my own form of observance, define and embrace a personal concept of God, or combine tenets of several different religions. However, according to traditional Jewish law, I am still considered Jewish.

And when my time is up, even if I don't know the first thing about the history of Judaism, the literature of the Old Testament, or the difference between *Hanukkah* and *harmonica*, I can be buried as a Jew.

The problem with all this is that it causes a lot of confusion to non-Jewish observers. For example, if I have a Jewish friend who is very observant, attends synagogue services every day, always covers his or her head with some kind of hat, recites prayers periodically throughout the day for myriad activities, keeps a strictly kosher home, and never works on the Sabbath, my friend will be considered a more *observant* Jew than I am. However, I am just as much a Jew as my friend is.

Many of the customs, procedures, beliefs, and behavioral aspects of the Jewish religion date back hundreds and even thousands of years. Most Jews throughout history lived in small, closed communities or ghettos and did not mix with general society, except perhaps for work or mercantile purposes. Today, of course, this is not true, especially in the United States (although there are always exceptions).

Thus, describing what it is like to be Jewish is like describing snow. While you can describe snow in terms of intensity, duration, wetness or dryness, inches of snowfall, historical perspectives, granularity, color, effect on visibility, and even the possibilities of school closings and ski conditions, you can also just say, "It's snowing."

It is really the range or spectrum of Jewishness that makes it difficult to describe or explain. An Israeli friend of mine describes it as a continuum. You can go from the ultra-Orthodox Jew all the way to the most liberal Reform Jew, from the extremist to the virtually nonobservant Jew, and still find some similarities of belief. Even though there are more differences than commonalities, all of these people are Jews. While there may be very little that ties them together (even tradition is not a leveling factor),

what they do have is a common lineage and a common ances-
try—a common history.

When describing things Jewish, I often find myself saying things like, "Some Jews believe . . . " or "Reform Jews do not believe . . ." or "It is not uncommon for some Jews to . . ." The reason for all this hedging is that Jews typically do not agree on many aspects of what is means to be Jewish or of Judaism itself. That doesn't mean, however, that I can't give you an overview, a snapshot, or perhaps a sketch of the Jewish way of life—the customs and beliefs, the holidays and festivals, the history and people.

In many instances throughout the book, I introduce a term in one section and more fully explain it in a later chapter. Hebrew and Yiddish words are defined in the glossary along with their correct pronunciations.

Christians
and Jews

Going to Church: The Jewish Roots of Christian Worship

L ike my parents, I was born in Brooklyn, New York. Like many other post–World War II families, mine moved to the suburbs when I was just an infant. However, for many years, we made a weekly pilgrimage to my grandparents' Brooklyn home in the heart of a commercial and residential neighborhood.

It was in this city atmosphere that I first experienced multi-culturalism at its best. On the streets were people of all racial and ethnic backgrounds, speaking a variety of languages—Italian, Polish, Yiddish, German, Greek, and Russian. Churches and synagogues dotted the neighborhoods, and since we generally visited on Saturday or Sunday, the sidewalks were often filled with families on their way to or from religious services. I observed ministers, rabbis, priests, and nuns (dressed in full habits) on their way to wherever they were going.

My father clearly remembers a nun speaking a few words of Yiddish to him as a boy when his Italian friends introduced him. Not unlike multilingual shopkeepers in ethnic neighborhoods today, many immigrant Jewish shopkeepers learned to speak enough Italian to do business with their customers. New York was truly a melting pot of sights, sounds, smells, tastes, and humanity.

It was natural, perhaps, that I would develop a fascination for different religions. In elementary school, my "girlfriend's" father was a pastor. In high school, one of my best friends was Catholic—an Irish Catholic, to be exact. I always marveled at the dramatic change in his behavior when we would pass a nun on the street or walk near his church. He talked to me about the confessional, the sermons, and the catechism. I once took him to sit in on Jewish religious class and laughed at the sight of him wearing a *kippah*.

The first time I attended a Mass was when a Jewish friend of mine from college married a Catholic woman. Since then, I've attended services at churches of many different Christian denominations; the rituals, sermons, and music have always held my attention.

While traveling in Spain, Italy, France, the Czech Republic, and elsewhere in Europe, as well as in Mexico and South America, my wife and I have visited magnificent cathedrals and small, intimate churches. I make it a habit to stay and observe religious services when I can. As a musician, I always marvel at the organ and choir music.

In preparing to write this book, I asked friends to allow me to join them at local church services. I wanted to know which elements of Christian worship came directly or indirectly from Jewish worship. How were the services alike?

During my church service attendance, research, observation, and communications with knowledgeable religious leaders, laypeople, and writers, I've become familiar with a few of the principal features of worship that Jews and Christians share.

First and foremost, we worship the same God—the God of the Hebrew Scriptures, the God of Abraham, the God who brought the children of Israel out of slavery in Egypt. This is the God who gave us the Ten Commandments. This is the God who Moses worshipped. It is the same God who Jesus worshipped. This came clearly into focus when I visited the Sistine Chapel in Rome: on one great wall, Michelangelo painted scenes from the life of Jesus, and on the opposite wall, he presented scenes from the life of Moses.

When they pray, both Christians and Jews give thanks to God and recite the works of God, recalling what God has done.

Worship services follow a certain sequence. Christians use the Latin word *ordo* to describe their worship sequence; Jews use the Hebrew word *seder* (or *siddur*). These words mean "order." The order of the services is different, which is to be expected considering the many hundreds of years during which religious practices developed and holiday calendars were modified. (This is the case for Christian holidays that may have once paralleled Jewish holidays, such as Easter and Lent, which have been connected to Passover.)

Both Jewish and Christian services begin with a "call to prayer." This is followed by prayers, recitation of portions of the Hebrew Scriptures, and readings from the Psalms. Christian services I've attended have included readings from Isaiah and the book of Kings.

In Jewish services, a portion from the Torah is read on the Sabbath as well as during other weekly services (see "The Torah and the Law"). In Christian services, there is a reading from one of the Gospels, the books that narrate the life and present the teachings of Jesus.

At some point in the Jewish service, the rabbi delivers a sermon. If a Torah portion has been read during the service, the sermon generally incorporates an idea or message from that portion. In the Christian service, a minister or priest delivers a sermon or homily in a similar manner, offering an understanding of the Scripture reading and an application to contemporary life and the community. (Many of the priests and ministers I've heard have a good sense of humor, as do most rabbis I've met. I guess it goes with the job.)

While attending Christian religious services, I have found some Christian prayers and blessings that closely parallel those included in Jewish services. For example, here is a prayer from Christian worship that may also be sung as a hymn; this prayer has its roots in Isaiah 6:3:

Holy, Holy, Holy, Lord God of power and might,
Heaven and earth are full of your glory . . .
Blessed is he who comes in the name of the Lord.

Here is the portion Jews recite in English (or sing in Hebrew) on the Sabbath and at other services:

Holy, Holy, Holy is the God of all being.
The whole earth is filled with Your glory.
Source of our strength, Sovereign God, how majestic is Your
presence in all the earth.

Praised be the glory of God in heaven and earth. *(Gates of Prayer)*

Here is another important part of the worship service that is similar in both the Christian and the Jewish traditions. For Christians, it is the Lord's Prayer:

Our Father, who art in heaven,

Hallowed be thy name.

Thy Kingdom come,

Thy will be done,

On earth as it is in heaven

Give us this day our daily bread.

And forgive us our trespasses,

as we forgive those who trespass against us.

And lead us not into temptation,

but deliver us from evil.

For thine is the kingdom, the power, and the glory.

For ever and ever. Amen

During their religious services, Jews recite the Kaddish several times. As with other parts of Sabbath worship services, the Kaddish is not a prayer per se; it extols the glory and name of God, but it does not ask for anything. While the theology behind the Kaddish is very different from that behind the Lord's Prayer, look at the similarity:

Let the glory of God be extolled, and God's great name be hallowed in the world whose creation God willed. May

God rule in our own day, our own lives, and the life of all
Israel, and let us say: Amen.

Let God's great name be blessed for ever and ever.

Beyond all praises, songs, and adorations that we can utter is
the Holy One, the Blessed One, whom yet we glorify,
honor, and exalt. And let us say: Amen.

For us and for all Israel, may the blessing of peace and the
promise of life come true, and let us say: Amen.

May the One who causes peace to reign in the high heavens,
cause peace to reign among us, all Israel, and all the
world, and let us say: Amen. *(Gates of Prayer)*

As both Jews and Christians know, bread and wine are common to both religions, but in very different ways. For centuries, Jews have been accustomed to making blessings over bread and wine, both in the synagogue and at mealtime at home with friends and family. At the end of a Jewish service, the leader or members of the congregation recite the blessings.

According to the Gospels, at the Last Supper, Jesus inaugurated and defined a rite that is central to Christian belief and to church services, the Eucharist. Here is the passage from Matthew 26:26–28:

> While they were eating, Jesus took a loaf of bread, and
> after blessing it he broke it, gave it to the disciples, and
> said, "Take, eat; this is my body." Then he took a cup,
> and after giving thanks he gave it to them, saying,
> "Drink from it, all of you; for this is my blood of the

covenant, which is poured out for many for the forgiveness of sins."

I have observed the solemnity with which churchgoers receive
communion, the rite that has links to the Jewish ritual consumption of bread and wine and to the temple sacrifices in
ancient Jerusalem. I also have learned that a key to understanding the Eucharist is in Jesus' command, "Do this in remembrance
of me" (Luke 22:19).

Water is an important part of both Jewish and Christian rituals.
In Judaism, water is used for conversion as well as for cleansing
and renewal, and it is usually linked to the use of the mikvah,
the ritual bath (see "Shabbat—The Sabbath"), although immersion can take place in any body of moving water (the Jordan
River, for example). There is evidence that the mikvah was being
used in the first century CE, and evidence of a mikvah bath is
found at the ruins of Masada (see "Israel"). The idea of using
a bath and immersion in water as a means of repentance was used
in ancient times and is common today to cleanse and prepare
for prayer.

In Christianity, water is used in the baptism ritual, which is
the sacrament of regeneration and admission into the Christian
community. In this manner, the person being baptized receives
a new and spiritual life. A baptism can be performed with symbolic sprinkling of or actual immersion in water.

Christianity and Judaism share many roots—in worship,
liturgy, and rituals. Of course, there remain much controversy
and grounds for scholarly debate about two thousand years of

history, belief, and learning. But I will leave the debate, research, and controversy to the scholars and end with a blessing common to both the Jewish and Christian traditions.

I have heard the Priestly Blessing recited by rabbis at synagogue services for my entire life, and I hear it now at many of the church services I attend. Also known as the Aaronic Benediction, it is the blessing of the Lord with which Aaron and his sons were to bless the children of Israel (Numbers 6:24–26):

> The LORD bless you and keep you;
> the LORD make his face to shine upon you, and be gracious
>   to you;
> the LORD lift up his countenance upon you, and give you
>   peace.

Jews, Jesus, and Christianity

Most modern Jews would agree that Jesus was a great man, a teacher, and even a prophet who traveled the land performing wonderful, miraculous deeds and preached love and kindness. Christians recognize Jesus as Christ, the Son of God, their savior, and the Messiah.

The Jewish people believe that when the Messiah comes there will be an end to world suffering. They look to Isaiah 2:4, which says, "they shall beat their swords into plowshares, and their spears into pruning hooks; nation shall not lift up sword against nation, neither shall they learn war any more." When the Messiah comes, the world will no longer be a place of hunger, hatred, and injustice, and the wolf, lamb, lion, and calf will all live together. Jews do not believe, therefore, that the Messiah has come, and they do not recognize Jesus as their savior or as the Son of God.

Thus, Jews who believe in either the coming of the Messiah or a messianic age continue to await the event, while Christians await the *second* coming of their Messiah.

Fortunately, there are signs of growing understanding, respect, and acceptance among many members of the Jewish and Christian faiths. Recent affirmations between leaders of Catholic and Jewish groups indicate agreement that both faiths are beloved of God and assured of God's grace. In many communities, interfaith councils and coalitions of religious congregations work to promote and maintain religious tolerance, mutual support, political action, and education.

If Jews are permitted to believe what they believe, and Christians are permitted to believe what they believe, all will benefit. History has shown that when one group forces their beliefs on another, serious problems occur.

Because of the nature of American society, many Christians and Jews work together, socialize, live in the same neighborhoods, and send their children to the same schools. If a Christian attends a synagogue service for a bar or bat mitzvah, a wedding, or a funeral service, he or she will recognize or be comfortable with many of the things being said. After all, such ceremonies use the same prayers and the same books of Moses that Jesus once studied. When Jews attend the church of a friend for a confirmation, wedding, funeral, or first communion, it's a little different; as guests they will not take communion, kneel, cross themselves, or actively participate in the Christian New Testament liturgy. It is foreign to their beliefs to do so. Many Bible stories, prayers, and psalms, however, are familiar to them.

Fortunately, Christians and Jews begin their relationship with several things in common: the Hebrew Scriptures (the Old Testament), the Ten Commandments, a Sabbath day, the importance of charitable giving, and similar versions of what is known as the golden rule. Most important, we share the same God.

During interfaith services, and when attending community services in response to local, national, and international disasters or tragedies, Christians and Jews as well as members of other faiths find themselves praying together. Under such circumstances, members of all faiths seem to rise to the occasion, focus on what they have in common, and worship together.

I hope that we continue to look to our similarities instead of our differences, and I pray that someday we all live together in peace, or as we say in Hebrew, *shalom*.

The Jewish
Religion

From Orthodox . . .

Until the early nineteenth century, virtually every Jew was an observant Jew as we would describe one today. A Polish Jew and a Persian Jew would follow similar rituals, even though the former might be described as Ashkenazic (originating from Eastern Europe) and the latter as Sephardic (originating from Spain, Southern Europe, the Near East, or North Africa (see "Ashkenazic and Sephardic Jews").

Orthodox Judaism resists change of its beliefs and practices. A central tenet of Orthodox Judaism is that the law of God was given to Moses on Mount Sinai, and the Torah, therefore, is divine. Thus, no law derived from the Torah should be tampered with, regardless of modern lifestyles, needs, or changes in society. Because of this, Orthodox rabbis believe that rulings of other Jewish groups are based on a different set of guidelines and are therefore not valid.

As in any group, in Orthodox Judaism, there is a range of beliefs and teachings, from ultra-Orthodox (see "Hasidim and

Hasidism") to more modern or centrist Orthodox. However, the traditional body of Jewish writings and the codification of law and practice remain the basis for belief, practice, and decision making, regardless of changes in modern life or personal conscience.

There are many rules that govern the practice of Judaism. An Orthodox Jew must learn these rules, which is no simple task, and keeping a given rule is not optional; that person must decide how best to apply the rule.

Since Orthodox Jews traditionally do not travel by car on the Sabbath, their synagogues generally are located within walking distance of home. Thus, while the congregations may be small, there are a significant number of them. The Orthodox Union, founded one hundred years ago, serves as the central organization for affiliated member synagogues in North America. Besides serving as a central coordinating organization, the Orthodox Union provides educational and social services, programs, and activities. There are more than one thousand affiliated and independent Orthodox Jewish congregations in the United States.

To Reform . . .

After the French Revolution and other political and social movements across the globe, many Jews began to modify certain religious and ceremonial practices, and a new movement in Judaism emerged. The principal and innovative difference was the belief that the Bible was not divine. From this major alteration in philosophy came changes in the rituals and practices of Judaism, some quite drastic (at one point, some Jews even celebrated the Sabbath on Sunday instead of Saturday).

Religious services began to be conducted in the local language instead of strictly in Hebrew; men and women were seated together; musical instruments provided accompaniment to the cantor and congregation; and restrictions on diet and on Sabbath activities were relaxed.

The Reform movement originated in Germany during the early nineteenth century. It then began to flourish among German Jewish immigrants to the United States. The Union of American Hebrew Congregations estimates that approximately one and a half million Reform Jews are now affiliated with more than nine hundred congregations in North America.

Today, Reform Judaism is a combination of traditional practice and modification of that practice, and it emphasizes a need to interpret the Jewish tradition from a modern and individual perspective. Complete equality of the genders is the rule, and many female rabbis and cantors lead Reform congregations. (My second marriage was performed by a female rabbi and a female cantor.) New chants, hymns, and melodies are continually added to the traditional prayers and sacred music of worship services, and these prayers are written in language that is gender-neutral.

While at one time the Reform movement did away with traditional prayer garb, it now encourages worshippers to follow their own beliefs and to wear prayer shawls and head coverings if they wish to do so.

Reform Judaism places decisions regarding rituals and observances more on the individual than Orthodox or Conservative Judaism does. With this individual religious autonomy, many Reform Jews shape a spiritual life for themselves by choosing from among the many holidays, rituals, and "rules" and by finding, over a period of time, which ones allow them to lead the Jewish life and lifestyle that is most comfortable for them. One rabbi I know stresses "informed choice": first study, then choose.

To Conservative . . .

In the late nineteenth century, there was a large increase in the Jewish population in the United States as a result of immigration from Russia and Eastern Europe. Not all of these Jewish immigrants were happy or comfortable with the Reform movement. Eventually, a schism occurred between the more traditional and the more "radical" leaders, and in the early twentieth century, this breakup led eventually to the Conservative movement in Judaism. The United Synagogues of Conservative Judaism estimates that today there are approximately eight hundred affiliated Conservative congregations representing some one and a half million members.

Conservative Judaism represents a mix of both traditional and more modern views. It accommodates the needs of Jewish life in contemporary society but at the same time accepts the divine inspiration of the law of the Torah. For example, it's OK to drive to the synagogue. This is because of the difference in lifestyles in the United States versus the traditional small Eastern European

Jewish communities of a hundred or more years ago. Today, the need to get to the synagogue on Shabbat from a distance too far to walk overrides the prohibition of "lighting a fire" (starting the car ignition).

The emphasis of Conservative belief lies between the Reform and the Orthodox. Personal decisions are based not as much on individual conscience as on the accepted practice of the Jewish community, the ritual committees within each congregation, and the guidance of Jewish scholarship through the ages. Conservative Judaism thus tends to be more traditional than Reform Judaism in its services, practices, and beliefs. However, some Conservative congregations appear more "reform" than some Reform congregations and vice versa, and it is not uncommon to find many Conservative congregants quite orthodox in their religious behavior and practices.

To Reconstructionist

Many people in the general population may not have heard of the Reconstructionist movement. It was inspired by the vision of Rabbi Mordecai Kaplan, a faculty member of a Conservative rabbinical seminary who helped found a new rabbinical college at the urgings of his students and supporters. Kaplan's concept was that Judaism is more than just a religion; it is a "civilization" that evolves and progresses and must therefore be "reconstructed"—rediscovered, and reinterpreted on an ongoing basis—to be kept alive.

In much the same manner as contemporary Conservative and Reform congregations, Reconstructionist congregations embrace a wide variety of traditional and nontraditional Jewish backgrounds, experiences, and lifestyles, and they operate in a gender-neutral environment. The Reconstructionist congregation often decides how it will honor traditional Jewish customs, molding them to accommodate what it considers the realities of modern life.

While Reconstructionist Jews have a strong commitment to tradition, they also search for contemporary meaning in the liturgy and religious service. If a particular Jewish custom is questionable in view of contemporary society, it will be examined and "reconstructed"; new meanings will be found in the old forms or they will be developed into more meaningful, innovative practices.

Reconstructionism diverges from Conservative and Reform Judaism in how it views the interpretation of traditional Jewish law and in how far Jewish law can be amended. Reconstructionism also differs from Conservative and Reform Judaism in its concept of ethical monotheism and its belief that the basic tenets of Judaism need to be reexamined and restated for our age. In general, Reconstructionist congregations fall somewhere between Reform and Conservative in terms of religious practice; they may be described as liberal in their ideology. As with many aspects of Judaism, there is a considerable range of practice and belief within the Reconstructionist movement.

The Jewish Reconstructionist Federation lists more than one hundred congregations in North America. A number of these congregations are organized as *havurot*. A *havurah* (singular) is a gathering of Jews who meet to worship and study together. The *havurah* is a religious group, but it also functions as a fellowship group and an extended family (see "Contemporary Synagogues and Congregations").

Although Reconstructionist congregations tend to be small, the concepts and philosophy of the movement have affected modern Jewish belief and practice.

Contemporary Synagogues
and Congregations

As the nature of society has changed in modern times, so have the Jewish community and, consequently, the synagogue. At one time, Jews lived in small *shtetlach* (singular *shtetl;* Yiddish for ghettos, villages, or settlements), closed communities in Eastern Europe or elsewhere. This is generally no longer the case in the United States, except for a few Hasidic communities located in New York and other cities. As Jews became more assimilated into mainstream society, the Jewish community became more disseminated, and Jews now live almost everywhere. As a result, the synagogue has become a place of gathering for Jewish people, a center not only for prayer and study but also for sharing heritage and culture, socializing, and growing within the faith.

The word *synagogue* derives from a Greek word that means "to congregate or to gather together." Evidence has been discovered of synagogues from two thousand years ago. Some congregations call their institution a synagogue, while others call it a temple, a word derived from Latin. The use of the word *temple* may refer to or be a symbolic reminder of the original temples of Jerusalem that were destroyed centuries ago (see "The Temple").

Through the years, synagogues have been built everywhere Jewish people live. Many reflect the architecture of the times or a country's specific style, whether baroque, Gothic, art deco, or contemporary/modern.

Some Jewish groups simply call themselves a congregation, while others refer to the synagogue as a *shul*, which is a Yiddish word that means "school." Still others organize and support a local community center, which provides a place for community events, nursery or other schools, youth activities, adult education, and often Shabbat services.

It is not necessary that a congregation have a full-time rabbi and/or cantor on the payroll to function. Often, a small congregation runs its worship services, religious school, and social functions with volunteers or with part-time or occasional "professional" help.

The word *havurah* refers to a small group that functions either independently of a larger religious congregation or as part of an organized synagogue. The word comes from the Hebrew root word for "friend." The havurah serves as a fellowship group and extended family with which to celebrate holidays, share support in times of crisis, enjoy religious and nonreligious events, and maintain a network of people who share the faith.

In addition, there are "alternative" congregations or organizations that combine Jewish traditions and beliefs with mysticism, vegetarianism, New Age philosophy, or social and political action. For example, Jewish meditation, spirituality, and education combine to form the basis of a very popular Jewish community group where I live in Northern California's Bay Area.

In other words, there is more than one place for Jewish people to meet, study, socialize, solve problems large and small, and worship.

A Personal Observation

I grew up in the 1950s and early 1960s attending a Conservative congregation. As any child brought up in a system, I believed that this was the norm in the same way that I thought my household was the norm and my high school was the norm and my rock-and-roll band was the norm and my mom and dad were the norm. As I matured, I was often shocked to discover that not only are things different out in the real world but also there is oftentimes no norm.

In my synagogue, it was typical for men and boys to wear a *kippah* (skullcap) when in the synagogue, to wear a *tallit* (prayer shawl) when attending religious services, and to recite certain prayers in Hebrew and others in English. At the time, few adult women in the congregation participated in leading religious services. However, more than ever before, girls were attending Hebrew school and participating in the bat mitzvah ritual, just as the boys celebrated their bar mitzvah. (The girls were the ones from whom I copied my Hebrew school homework.)

The first time I attended a Reform Shabbat service, I was quite surprised. For the most part, the congregants did not wear a *kippah* or *tallit;* much more of the service was in English than in Hebrew; and when the rabbi read the Torah portion, he translated it into English, line by line, as he went along—I liked this method since it meant I did not have to read the English to know what he was talking about.

Through the years, I have belonged to more than one Reform congregation, and I have generally found the services stimulating and informative. I have also attended Conservative services reminiscent of the synagogue of my youth as well as Orthodox services, which reflect traditional Judaism as it has been practiced for centuries. On occasion I've attended what I would refer to as "alternative" congregations and taken part in services that were outside my own definition of *mainstream.* I did note, however, the joy and delight with which the congregants participated, and I respected their enthusiasm.

My search for a religious or spiritual life has been a dynamic process. The spirituality I desired in my youth changed as I matured. Marriage and children affected my decisions about the type of religion my family and I sought and the degree to which we sought it. As I entered middle age, I found myself looking once more for a meaningful spiritual life, one that maybe was quite different from what I previously wanted or needed.

With its vast sources of ritual and history, Judaism provides each Jewish person with a wealth of options for how best to shape his or her spirituality. Basic to Judaism is a belief in the one God and the wisdom of the Torah. In the words of the prophet Micah (6:8), "what does the Lord require of you but to do justice, and to love kindness, and to walk humbly with your God?"

Finally, the scholar and teacher Hillel was inspired by Leviticus 19:18 ("you shall love your neighbor as yourself") when he said, "The entire Law [Torah] may be reduced to one statement, 'What is hateful to you, do not do to your neighbor,' the remainder being but commentary on this fundamental principle." In this statement, both he and Jesus, certainly inspired by the same Scripture, were in total agreement.

Inside the Synagogue

The Torah and the Law

If you have ever been to a synagogue service or seen parts of a service on television or in a movie, you know that Jews read from a scroll. This scroll is the Torah. In this day of sophisticated word processing and print technology, a highly trained scribe (*sofer* in Hebrew) still produces each scroll by hand. The sofer writes on parchment using a quill and special ink in the same way and to the same exacting standards as has been done for centuries.

Specifically, the Torah refers to the Five Books of Moses (the Pentateuch). Sometimes, however, people may use the word *Torah* in a general sense to refer to the entire Bible or to all the religious texts of the Jewish people.

The phrase "the Jewish Bible" refers to three distinct groups of Jewish writings. First is the Torah (the Pentateuch). These are the Five Books of Moses (Genesis, Exodus, Leviticus, Numbers, and Deuteronomy), recorded on the Torah scroll as described previously. Portions are read each week during synagogue services.

The second section is known as the Prophets (in Hebrew, *Nevi'im*) and includes the Books of Joshua, Judges, Samuel I and II, Kings I and II, Isaiah, Jeremiah, Ezekiel, and the twelve minor prophets, which count as one book (Hosea, Joel, Amos, Obadiah, Jonah, Micah, Nahum, Habakkuk, Zephaniah, Haggai, Zechariah, and Malachi).

The third section is variously known as the Writings, the Hagiographa, or *Ketuvim,* a Hebrew word. This section includes the books of Psalms, Proverbs, Job, Song of Songs, Ruth, Lamentations, Ecclesiastes, Esther, Daniel, Ezra and Nehemiah (these count as one book), and Chronicles I and II.

Using the first letters of the word Torah and the Hebrew words for the other two books (*Nevi'im* and *Ketuvim*), you arrive at the acronym TNK, which is pronounced "Tanakh" and is what Jewish people call the Bible (the Holy Scriptures) in Hebrew.

Many of the laws, passages, and directives in the Torah are not fully explained, are confusing, or may seem contradictory. Over the centuries, law based upon study and analysis of the Torah was passed down by word of mouth. This oral law, which provided explanations and amplifications of the written law, was finally organized and written down by the earliest rabbinic scholars in the first through third centuries CE and is known as the *Mishnah* (Hebrew for "recapitulation"). The Mishnah deals with temple rituals, holiday observances, agricultural issues, and family life, but it also contains many proverbs and philosophical observations.

As scholars studied the Mishnah, they wrote down their commentaries and discussions about it. These commentaries, called the *Gemara* (Aramaic for "study"), are interspersed into each paragraph or section of the Mishnah and give insight into historical, spiritual, ethical, and legal issues.

The combination of the Mishnah and the Gemara is called the Talmud. In case you're not already confused, there are two versions of the Talmud: the Jerusalem (or Palestinian) Talmud and the Babylonian Talmud. These days, when we refer to the Talmud, we refer to the Babylonian Talmud, which was completed in about 500 CE. Talmudic study, while quite difficult, opens a world of spiritual wisdom, humor and anecdote, and rabbinical arguments and puzzles.

As a matter of fact, the Talmud is a storehouse of advice, recommending that we always begin a lecture with a funny story, that we should never have more than twenty-five students in a classroom, and that we should always give a person the benefit of the doubt. It also gives practical advice for otherwise arguable situations. For example, when is Shabbat over? The answer is at the end of the day, when it is dark. How dark must it be for the day to be ended? The Talmud tells us that a person must be able to see three stars in the sky. But what if it is a rainy or overcast night? Consult the Talmud for the solution.

Throughout the ages, many illustrious and renowned Jewish scholars have contributed to the oral tradition, the Mishnah and the Talmud, and the Midrash, a collection of rabbinical questions and commentaries on the Bible (for example, "Why did God appear to Moses as a burning bush and not a tree?"). *Midrash* is a Hebrew word meaning "investigation," and passages in the Midrash often take the form of a story about whatever issue is being discussed or explained.

It is not unusual to refer to this group of rabbinical scholars as a source of information or authority when describing a particular law or practice in Judaism. Some people believe that the first rabbis were the Pharisees, a Jewish group that lived in the Holy Land at the time of Jesus. Their interpretation of the Torah was liberal for that day, and they introduced new ideas and concepts that were contrary to much of what was believed at the time. For the next thousand years, these scholars, teachers, and philosophers—collectively referred to as "the Rabbis" or "the Sages"—worked on the religious books and documents that form the core of Jewish religious writings.

The entire body of Jewish law is known as *Halachah*, and it is this law that guides observant Jews through life, indicating what should be done at any given time or in a given situation as well as what should not be done and what is not acceptable. In other words, Halachah indicates patterns for behavior and for life in general. The root of the word *Halachah* means "to go" or "to walk," and Halachah can be thought of as a person's "path through life." Halachah, therefore, is a set of codes based on the Talmud that regulates family relationships, legal matters, education, diet, and personal and religious observances.

During the many years when Jews were self-governed in their own communities, these codes provided a legal system, which was a guide to what was acceptable and what was punishable as a crime. After Jews were no longer subject to the discipline of their own community, the law of the land in which they lived took precedence, but the Halachah lived on as a guide to personal behavior.

Modern Jews continue to seek spiritual guidance as well as practical advice from their rabbis and scholars, just as people of other religious groups seek help and advice from their pastors, ministers, and priests. While the Jewish tradition of law and commentaries on the Torah may not always be followed to the letter, these sources, spanning thousands of years and written and collected by the great minds of the ages, provide a wealth of guidance and wisdom from the past to be used in the present.

Issues covered by these writings vary in depth and importance, from marriage to divorce, from kosher kitchen practices to experimental scientific research, and from smoking in or near the synagogue to the introduction of female rabbis and cantors in congregations. Whatever the question or issue, Jewish tradition, wisdom, and scholarship can often help solve contemporary problems. While members of the different branches of Judaism follow these sources to different degrees (or not at all), they can be spiritual (as well as secular) guides if we wish them to be.

Prayers and Blessings

Any Jew can pray on his or her own. However, to say certain prayers or to have what is considered a full worship service, there must be at least ten adults present. This group is called a minyan. The requirements for being a member of a minyan vary among different congregations.

Orthodox congregations require that the minyan comprise ten Jewish *men* over age thirteen. Most Conservative congregations include women in the ten-person minyan. Reform congregations generally do not require a minyan for group prayer.

It is considered somewhat of an honor to be the tenth person to join the group, since then the group can get to the business at hand. I remember occasions when someone had to go hustle up a tenth member, often calling someone on the phone or snatching a person from his office.

The number ten appears quite a few times in Judaism: ten commandments, ten plagues, Abraham's ten tests of faith, the ten righteous in Sodom and Gomorrah, and so forth. The congregation of "ten" comes from the Book of Numbers: ten of Moses' spies, returning from the Land of Canaan, had distorted the truth, whereupon God proclaims, "How long shall this wicked congregation complain against me?" (Numbers 14:27).

In services where we read from the Torah, it is customary that when the Torah "stands" (is held or raised), the congregants stand; when the Torah sits (is placed on the reading lectern or returned to the ark), the congregants may sit. Whenever the ark containing the Torah scrolls is open or when the scrolls are being carried, the congregants stand. There are some exceptions, but those are the general rules. Your physical abilities and health take precedence over these rules.

Traditional Orthodox Jews pray in the morning, in the afternoon, and again in the evening (although the afternoon and evening prayers are often said in succession). Depending on how observant they are, other Jews may pray once a day, once a month, once a year, or only when they feel the need to express happiness, grief, or some other emotion.

I was always under the impression that a person "faces east" when praying. In actuality, a person faces toward Jerusalem, specifically toward the site where the temple once stood. Thus, if you are in Turkey, you look at your compass and face south.

There are several prayers that are common to most services. The first (from Deuteronomy 6:4) is the Shema, an affirmation that announces, "Hear, O Israel!: The Lord is our God, the Lord is one."

Liberal Jewish congregations now translate prayers so that they are gender-sensitive. Here is such a version of the same prayer:

Hear, O Israel: the Eternal One is our God, the Eternal God alone! Blessed is God's glorious majesty for ever and ever!

A second prayer basic to the service is the Amidah, generally recited silently while standing. In this prayer we ask God to give us peace and help us solve many of the personal problems and difficulties we all face.

The Aleinu is a prayer that looks to the future as one of hope and peace while reminding us that it is incumbent upon us to give praise to God.

The Kaddish prayer, extolling God's majesty and kingdom, is recited several times during a service. Although having nothing to do with death, the Kaddish is traditionally recited while remembering the departed. As I get older, I hear (and recite) this prayer more and more as friends and relatives die.

As you might expect, there are blessings for everyday routines, such as waking, eating, traveling, and retiring for the day. Most common is the Grace before Meals, known as the *Motzi* or *HaMotzi*. This prayer gives thanks for the "bread of the earth," bread being symbolic of food in general:

We praise You, Eternal God, Sovereign of the universe, for You cause bread to come forth from the Earth.

Another standard blessing is the blessing over wine, the *Kiddush*, giving thanks for "the fruit of the vine":

We praise You, Eternal God, Sovereign of the universe,
Creator of the fruit of the vine.

There is also a prayer of Grace after Meals as well as one that is recited before lighting the Shabbat candles.

After thousands of years, you can imagine that special prayers have developed to respond to special needs. Some may be considered bizarre and some unnecessary. Others may actually seem inappropriate or objectionable in this day and age ("Thank you, God, for not having created me a woman" [see "Women and Judaism"]).

Do all Jews recite all of these prayers? Hardly. As I've said before, it all depends on a person's level of religious observance. Someone may use prayer time to offer up personal messages to God or to create his or her own individual devotions. However, the list of available prayers in Judaism is extensive.

Special prayers can be created for special needs. One special prayer thanks God for the creation of the rainbows. Or, remember the scene in *Fiddler on the Roof* when the townspeople ask the rabbi if there is a blessing for the czar? After a moment of reflection, the rabbi replies, "May the Lord bless and keep the czar . . . far away from us!"

Anyone who plays a reed instrument—clarinet, saxophone, oboe, or bassoon—knows the constant frustration of dealing with the fickle reeds. I once asked a rabbi if there could possibly be a blessing made over a saxophone reed or if this was a sacrilegious request. "Nonsense," he replied, and offered me a prayer using the Hebrew word for reeds, *zufim,* which is the word used to describe the Reed Sea. I use the blessing now and am always happy to share it with my fellow musicians. Reeds still drive me crazy, but the prayer thanks God for creating and giving us the reed, the bread, the fruit of the earth, the rainbow, or whatever. The quality of the gift is not the primary issue.

Symbols—The Mezuzah
and the Star of David

When you visit the homes of many Jews, you will find a small metal, wooden, glass, or ceramic case several inches in height called a *mezuzah* (literally, "doorpost") fastened to the right doorpost of the front door. Inside the mezuzah is a tiny handwritten parchment scroll (called a *klaf*) containing two paragraphs from the Torah (Deuteronomy 6:4–9 and 11:13–21) as well as three Hebrew letters that spell one of the names used for God.

The Bible instructs us to "write them [God's Words] on the doorposts of your house and on your gates" (Deuteronomy 6:9). As far back as two thousand years ago, Jews have chosen to follow this instruction using the mezuzah.

It is not uncommon for a person to kiss his or her fingertips and transfer the kiss to the mezuzah by touching it as he or she passes in and out of the home; others touch the mezuzah first and then kiss their fingers. Many Jews have only one mezuzah in their home, but some have them affixed to the doorway of each bedroom or living area in the house. Many people wear a small mezuzah on a chain around the neck as jewelry.

Like many customs, the fixing of the mezuzah is surrounded by tradition, mysticism, and a pinch of superstition. Some say the letters on the scroll make up an acronym that gives protection to the home. I know of a distinguished symphony conductor who delayed the move into his new house until the local rabbi could come to the home, certify that the scroll inside the mezuzah was proper, accurate, and legitimate, and conduct a formal ceremony at which time the mezuzah was applied to the doorpost. Many people take these things very seriously.

Another symbol often seen in pieces of jewelry is the *chai*, made up of two Hebrew letters. The word *chai* means "life," just as the phrase (and song title), "L'Chaim!" (often used as a toast) means "to life." In addition, the two letters making up the word *chai* have a numerical equivalent of eighteen, giving this number a special significance to Jews. Multiples of eighteen dollars are often given as gifts or donations.

The six-pointed star, often called the Star of David, is commonly associated with Jews and Judaism. In Hebrew it is known as the Magen David, which means the "shield of David." Ironically, this symbol has been associated throughout the centuries not only with Jews, but with Muslims, Christians, and other groups. However, as it came to be used more and more in the design of synagogues built in Europe over three hundred years ago, it became identified as a Jewish symbol. It was so closely identified with Judaism that Nazis forced Jews to wear a yellow Star of David during the years of persecution and incarceration.

Now, the Star of David not only decorates jewelry, gifts, and other Judaica but also adorns the flag of the State of Israel. Jews around the world consider the Star of David a proud symbol of Judaism.

The Role of the Rabbi

The word *rabbi* means "teacher," and teaching has been the job of the rabbi for almost two thousand years. Some rabbis through the ages have achieved great acclaim as a result of their wisdom, leadership, and holiness. The word *rabbi* can be used to mean "teacher" in venues other than religion; for example, a professional athlete might give homage to his mentor by saying, "He was my rabbi."

Modern American rabbis graduate from a rabbinical seminary after four to five years of graduate study. Each rabbi is ordained by the seminary from which he or she graduates.

As is the case in other modern religious groups, the role of the rabbi has changed through the years and now encompasses a greater degree of leadership, management, and counseling than ever before. It is reasonable to say that the rabbi sets the tone for the synagogue and congregation.

As representatives of their congregations and the Jewish faith, rabbis sometimes find themselves in positions of conflict. This might occur when the rabbi and the congregation that hired him or her disagree on volatile issues such as military conflicts, inter-marriage, and local community actions. The rabbi may believe that Jewish law or tradition calls for one particular action when the members of the congregation desire another. Thus, rabbis often have to walk a fine line. Since the rabbi is hired by the con-gregation and given a contract, this contract might not be renewed if the congregation is not pleased with the rabbi's deci-sions or behavior. Likewise, the rabbi can choose to go elsewhere at the end of the contract period.

Rabbis are encouraged to marry, and most lead normal per-sonal lives, except for the fact that they must often be available during times of need or crisis. They are actively involved in con-gregational activities, synagogue worship, and religious educa-tion. Rabbis often represent the Jewish view in community functions and take part in the many marriages, funerals, and other family events and crises that occur on a regular basis.

Above all, a rabbi is expected to be wise in the ways of Judaism, to be well versed in the Jewish tradition, to be com-passionate when dealing with human frailties and needs, and to live by a high ethical standard. Add to this the fact that many congregations expect the rabbi to have a great personality, give terrific sermons, and tell good (but not off-color) jokes, and you have a job that presents quite a challenge.

One of the most clever rabbis I ever met was able to deliver sermons that kept me on the edge of my chair, and he was witty beyond belief. The congregation, however, was not as apprecia-tive of him as I was, and his contract was not renewed. A rabbi in another congregation I attended was a very nice guy and was

loved by all the children; when his contract expired, he was lured
to a larger congregation in a bigger city and made the move in
much the same way as a free-agent ball player jumps from one
team to another. As a matter of fact, the rabbi of the congregation in which I grew up played minor league baseball before
choosing to enter the rabbinate and, for many years, was a
"ringer" on the synagogue softball team. He served the same
congregation for his entire career, was made rabbi emeritus on
his retirement, and was so honored until his death.

Just about all the rabbis I've known manage to tell good jokes
("A rabbi, a priest, and a chicken walk into a bar . . .").

The Role of the Cantor

David also commanded the chiefs of the Levites to
appoint their kindred as the singers to play on musical
instruments, on harps and lyres and cymbals, to raise
loud sounds of joy. (1 Chronicles 15:16)

Jewish worship has included music for thousands of years. Much of the synagogue religious service is sung or chanted. It is generally the role of the cantor to lead the congregation in these portions of prayer or to sing them him- or herself.

Thus, the cantor takes on the task of interpreting Jewish liturgy through music and song. While some of the Torah cantillations go back thousands of years, a song sung in an Israeli kibbutz or a children's camp may sometimes find its way into a joyous Sabbath or holiday celebration, and the cantor is often the person who introduces it. New melodies and choir pieces continue to be written by Jewish composers and introduced into the religious repertoire.

Much of what a cantor does is interpret Hebrew, a language that many congregants do not understand; the cantor makes Hebrew meaningful through music.

Both the Reform and the Conservative movements maintain five-year graduate programs in which prospective cantors pursue studies in religion and liturgical music and on graduation are invested as cantors. The role of the modern cantor (*hazzan* in Hebrew) often includes training children (or adults) for bar or bat mitzvah; performing administrative tasks; presiding at special synagogue events; directing choir, shows, and celebrations; and officiating or assisting at weddings, funerals, and other life-cycle, social and family events. Very often the cantor performs pastoral counseling as well.

Some cantors are operatically trained at music conservatories. The cantor of a congregation I once belonged to performed with our local symphony orchestra, and several opera stars have been cantors, including the late Richard Tucker of the Metropolitan Opera (by coincidence, he was the cantor at the synagogue in which my parents were married). While the cantor does not necessarily need to have a "great" voice, the Talmud does say that a cantor should have a "sweet" (aesthetically pleasing) voice. Part of his or her job is to inspire the congregation and help the congregants truly feel the prayer experience, not just listen to it.

Many cantors are employed full-time by their congregations, and others may work part-time. Sometimes, a qualified layperson fills the role of prayer leader during a religious service, but the title "cantor" is usually reserved for someone who has earned a degree and has been specifically trained for the profession.

One cantor I know feels very strongly that much like the job of any other religious leader, the job of cantor is not just a job, but a "religious calling," and in many ways, the cantor often inspires the spiritual and religious environment in a synagogue.

As a musician, during religious services I always try to sit on the side of the synagogue nearest the cantor. That's where the action is.

Jewish Education

In most societies today, a person's status in the community is determined by economics. The amount of money made or had; the home lived in; the vacations taken; the cars, clothing, jewelry, and miscellaneous "toys" possessed—all of these, along with fame and notoriety, are the indicators by which we judge a person's success. Not so in the traditional and historical Jewish community.

In the film *Fiddler on the Roof,* Tevye sings that he wishes to be a rich man. Why? True, he would like to dress his wife and family in fine clothes and have a big home with staircases going up and down and nowhere. However, for himself he longs for the time and freedom to sit and study all day in the synagogue and to command the respect of the men around him, something that only scholarship brings.

Through the ages, education and wisdom were the means of gaining status in the Jewish community. If a couple had a daughter to marry off, a young scholar who was knowledgeable in the ways of the Torah and the Talmud was often considered a more preferable suitor than a wealthy man.

In modern American Jewish communities, the standards are a little different. Jewish education for boys and girls often ends either after or within a few years after a bar or bat mitzvah. Secular, general education takes precedence over religious training. The traditional desire and respect for a religious education seem to have been redirected toward a good college education, often followed by graduate and/or professional studies.

In spite of this great emphasis on secular education, there are many institutions of Jewish learning in the United States. They range from Jewish elementary and day schools to Jewish high schools, colleges, and universities. Many Jewish institutions of higher learning are run by Orthodox or Hasidic groups or congregations, but this is not always the case. Regardless of their affiliation, these schools often attract students from more liberal Jewish backgrounds.

Sometimes parents choose a Jewish religious education for elementary or high school students because they consider the educational standards higher at a Jewish institution than at the local public schools. In this way, Jewish parents are not much different from non-Jewish parents who send their children to parochial or private elementary and high schools.

Along with Jewish seminaries for prospective rabbis and cantors, there are also independent religious colleges that offer joint degree programs with other colleges and universities (a Jewish religious college is called a *yeshiva*). In addition, there are universities that are either sponsored by or were founded by Jewish groups. Many public and private colleges and universities offer courses, programs, and, in some cases, degrees in Jewish studies or Hebrew.

On college campuses, student centers represent various religious groups. For Jewish students, there is the Hillel Center, which offers religious services, social programs, counseling, community service opportunities, and other activities.

For adults who yearn either to continue a previously interrupted Jewish education or to know more about Judaism and their Jewish heritage, there are many continuing or adult education classes offered through synagogues, Jewish community centers, and other organizations. These offerings encompass a wide range of Judaic subjects including language, literature, poetry, music, theater, film, history, religion, law, and politics. Although it is always possible for people to explore and study on their own, the Jewish tradition encourages study with a teacher as well as classroom study. I have enjoyed many hours of Torah study with the rabbi and a large group of adult students on Saturday mornings before worship services. The discussions are always lively, thought provoking, and remarkably fun.

Confirmation

Along with a bar or bat mitzvah, which generally takes place around the age of thirteen (see "An Invitation to a Bar Mitzvah and a Bat Mitzvah"), many Jewish teenagers also take part in a confirmation exercise when they are fifteen or sixteen. The confirmation celebrates their graduation from religious school and traditionally occurs around the holiday of Shavuot, the spring festival commemorating the deliverance of the Ten Commandments.

While Jewish confirmation services were originally introduced by the Reform movement as a substitute for the bar and bat mitzvah, it has now become an addition to these celebrations of adulthood and an opportunity for Jewish teenagers to mark another step in the continuation of their religious education.

Congregation Membership and Paying the Bills

Traditionally, Shabbat has not been a time for working, transacting business, or handling money (see "Shabbat—The Sabbath"). Therefore, unlike most Christian services, a collection plate or basket is not passed during Sabbath services. Since money is not collected at services, congregations are supported by congregation membership and the collecting of synagogue membership dues, donations for special purposes, and fund-raising events. Congregation membership is usually flexible, which allows people with limited or fixed incomes to join.

As you can imagine, synagogue buildings must be established, maintained, and repaired, and the rabbi, cantor, and other support personnel must be paid. The mortgage must be taken care of. If there is a religious school or day camp associated with the synagogue, it must be funded, and educators and administrators need to be employed (which is the same as any religious or parochial school).

Synagogues are democratic organizations. Each congregation nominates a board of directors, elects officers, and sets up various committees. Typically, a congregation includes education, ritual, and membership committees, as well as others that deal with fund-raising, social action, community outreach, and library issues. Often there is a group that aids members needing help after the death of a family member.

The synagogue generally belongs to one of the larger denominations—Orthodox, Conservative, Reform, or Reconstructionist—each of which maintains an organizational headquarters. If a newly formed congregation follows the principles and precepts of a particular movement, it will be accepted into the larger group and can use the group's resources for religious materials, educational curricula, social activities, and national publications. While a synagogue may be a member of a larger association of congregations, there is no organization similar to a Catholic archdiocese that supports individual synagogues.

More than ever before, congregations are called on to contribute to religious and social causes, and this is being done more frequently during religious services. How is this accomplished without money passing hands? Some congregations place pledge cards or envelopes on or near the seats of congregants, who are asked to return them sometime after Shabbat. In the end, each congregation determines when and how fund-raising occurs.

The Temple

There were actually two historical temples, both built on the same site in Jerusalem at different times in history. King Solomon built the First Temple around 950 BCE. For the Jews, it was a holy place. It contained a central room known as the Holy of Holies that housed the sacred Ark of the Covenant; this room was visited only by the high priest and only on one day a year—Yom Kippur (see "Jewish Priests"). Jews came to pray in the temple, and the priests offered animal sacrifices to God (the temple was the only place where this was supposed to be done).

The First Temple was destroyed by the Babylonians under King Nebuchadnezzar in 586 BCE, and the Jews were exiled. Temple worship did not resume until after the Persians defeated the Babylonians later in the sixth century BCE.

With the return of the Jewish exiles to Jerusalem, the temple was eventually restored around 516 BCE. The battle in which the Maccabees were victorious over Antiochus Epiphanes (circa 165

BCE) is commemorated by Hanukkah (see "Hanukkah—Is It Really the 'Jewish Christmas'?").

King Herod built the Second Temple on a grand scale around 30 BCE. According to the historian Flavius Josephus, who lived and wrote during this time, the temple appeared from the distance "like a mountain covered with snow; for any part not covered with gold was dazzling white."

The Second Temple was also destroyed, this time by the Romans in 70 CE under General Titus.

With the destruction of the First and Second Temples, the Jewish priesthood ended, as did the offering of animal sacrifices. The destruction also brought an end to the Jewish nation and a centuries-old way of life.

Although the Jewish people made numerous attempts to regain the Temple site, they were not permitted access to the devastated city for decades. Eventually, they migrated back to Jerusalem, where they dreamed and waited for the coming of the Messiah and the rebuilding of the holy city.

The ancient temple's Western Wall is one remnant of the temple that still stands. This wall is not actually part of the temple itself, but is a part of a retaining wall that surrounded the Temple Mount. As a symbol of the temple, however, it remains the most sacred site for Jewish people in Israel.

I have been privileged to stand at the wall and pray along with visitors from around the world. Being in Jerusalem felt very special, but standing at the Western Wall helped me feel closer to God.

Many Jews observe the holiday Tisha B'Av, also called the Day of Lamentation (see "Other Religious Events"). This holiday follows a three-week mourning period, which commemorates the destruction of the First and Second Temples. It is a day to fast and to mourn the loss of the temples as well as what they signified in Jewish history.

Jewish Priests

Many Jews have the surname Cohen or Cohn (other spellings abound), Kaplan, Katz, or variations of these. What most of these people have in common is that they are members of the *Kohanim*—the priests, and their names are derived from that Hebrew word.

During the sin of the Golden Calf (Exodus 32:4, 19–21; see also Cecil B. DeMille's film *The Ten Commandments*), the only ones who did *not* participate were the members of the tribe of Levi—the Levites or *Levi'im*. Moses and his brother, Aaron, were members of this tribe, and Aaron was later appointed the high priest. During the time of the temple in Jerusalem, Aaron's male descendants served as priests. Since that time, these descendants have continued to be recognized as Kohanim.

These "priests" do not serve in the same manner as priests do in the Catholic and Episcopal churches. In Orthodox and many Conservative congregations, the Kohanim perform in a number of religious rituals. On the High Holidays, for example, the priests gather to bless the congregation in a solemn and ancient procedure. In addition, when reading from the Torah, a *Kohen* is traditionally the first to receive an *aliyah* (see glossary). The Talmud proscribes certain technical rules that Kohanim must follow in regard to marriage and divorce.

The Levites' descendants, many of whom now have surnames such as Levy, Levine, and variations thereof, had the role of serving the priests in the temple. This included maintaining the sanctuary and performing other functions at a time when animal sacrifices were given to God. These practices ended with the destruction of the temple (see "The Temple").

Today, there is a ritual during the High Holidays and other biblical holidays when Levi'im help prepare the Kohanim, who then go on to bless the congregation. A Levi is traditionally given the second aliyah honor when the Torah is read during religious services. In the Israeli religious community, the Levi'im and the Kohanim take part in daily and life cycle ritual functions.

I want to emphasize that many modern Jews, although technically Levi'im or Kohanim, do not live the religious lives that their ancestors did and may not even be aware of the special roles or restrictions that apply to them.

Finally, if you're not a Levi or a Kohen, then you're an Israelite. That's what I am, and proud of it.

Time for Confession

While you may have thought that only Catholics confess their sins and are forgiven, there are prayers that observant Jews may say more than once a day that include the words, "Forgive us, for we have sinned."

Jews do not direct their confession to a priest as Catholics do. Jewish confession is directed instead to the party against whom a person has sinned. If we have transgressed against God, then we must repent, return to, and reconcile with God. As important as confession is, it is repentance that is truly important. We are expected to acknowledge a specific sin, rectify that sin if possible, regret our actions, and resolve to change our ways.

If we have sinned against another person, we must seek forgiveness first from the person whom we have wronged. Only then can God forgive us.

Personal confessions before marriage or on a person's deathbed have been common in the past. Today, however, these confessions are rare and do not need to be made before a rabbi (who does not, in any case, have the power to absolve sin).

There is a prayer, however, that we recite regularly in religious services; this prayer is an alphabetical list of confessions recited by the congregation as a whole—"We have sinned; we have stolen," and so on. While each congregant may not be guilty of the sins confessed, it is an opportunity to take responsibility for others who may be guilty and to acknowledge that none of us is without sin. During this prayer I tend to reflect on what I might have done recently that could be construed as sin or transgression against God or another person. I find it a sobering experience to evaluate my life and my behavior in this manner.

It is interesting to note that the word for *sin* in Hebrew does not translate as a terrible transgression or dastardly deed. It comes from a root word that means "to miss the mark," as in archery. Thus, a sin is defined in Judaism more as a missed opportunity, something you could have done or said, a kindness you could have expressed, or a righteous act you might have performed, but did not. Many of the sins described in the liturgy during the High Holidays are verbal sins—hurts caused by insult or slander, words spoken in anger or in an insulting manner. The only way to right these wrongs is to ask forgiveness of the person you have insulted, slandered, or attacked. In this manner you have turned away from your own sin and taken action, regardless of whether the person has forgiven you. What is important is that you confess sincerely and from the heart.

Who's in Charge?

Who's in charge of all the Jewish people? Who runs the show? Who is the "Jewish spokesperson," the one visited by American presidents and other heads of state when a comment or endorsement is needed from the Jewish community? Who sets the official Jewish policy for capital punishment, divorce, and birth control?

The answer is no one. There is no person equivalent to the pope or the archbishop of Canterbury. There are two chief rabbis in Israel, but their function is to make policy, settle disputes, and decide on religious matters regarding marriage, divorce, conversions, and the like—but only in Israel. They would never be considered spokespeople for world Judaism. I have no idea who they are, and I wouldn't know them if I bumped into them in a kosher deli.

In the United States, rabbis are considered teachers, representatives of their own congregations to the community, and, sometimes, scholars. However, the moment an individual rabbi claims to represent American Jews or even all the Jews in a particular city or state, beware! A credibility check is in order.

Of course, there are organizations that speak for large groups of Jews and monitor and publicly comment on anti-Semitism or controversial issues. Many Jewish educational and charitable agencies have large memberships and support or maintain schools, hospitals, and homes for the elderly and raise funds for Jewish or Israeli organizations. Very often, rabbis and synagogue leaders in a particular area will join together to protest a specific social issue, demonstrate against an anti-Semitic speaker or rally, or join with clergy from other denominations to support an effort to combat hunger, disease or social injustice.

But no. There is no Jewish pope.

Holidays
and Festivals

Holidays and
the Jewish Calendar

One of the problems that many non-Jews (and many Jews, for that matter) have with Jewish holidays is that they are "traveling" holidays. Unlike Christmas and New Year's Day, Jewish holidays occur on different dates each year. Why?

Jewish holidays are determined by the Jewish calendar, a calendar based on the lunar cycle. Today, most of the world uses the Gregorian calendar, which is based on the solar cycle of 365 days; the one leap year day every four years evens things out.

The Jewish calendar, though quite different, is very interesting. Based on the typical lunar cycle of 29 days, the length of Jewish months alternates between 29 and 30 days. If you multiply 12 months per year times 29.5 days, you get only 354 days. In former days, this "short" year was coordinated or synchronized with the solar year by adding a full month—actually a leap month—every two or three years. There are 7 leap months in a 19-year cycle. Thus, a "regular" Jewish year contains 353 to 355 days; but a Jewish year containing a leap month has 383 to 385 days. Because of this, the Jewish calendar and the Gregorian calendar are, more often than not, out of sync.

It was important to establish leap months in the Jewish calendar because the Torah specifies that the Passover holiday must occur in the spring. If there were no leap months, then the Jewish calendar would be similar to the Muslim calendar, by which a particular holiday, such as Ramadan, can occur during any season of the year.

The Jewish calendar, introduced in the fourth century CE, has been around a lot longer than the Gregorian calendar, which was instituted in the sixteenth century. The year 2000 (Gregorian) coincided with the year 5761 on the Jewish calendar. Simply add 3,761 years to our current year to get the Jewish year. Today, Jewish people use this calendar to determine religious holidays and to remember the anniversary of a death. The Jewish year date is also indicated on Jewish marriage contracts and other religious documents.

Each month of the Jewish calendar begins with the new moon, when the first sliver of moon is visible in the sky. Thus, there is a full moon on the fifteenth day of every month.

Before the introduction of modern communications systems, observers would report their sighting of the new moon to the proper authorities in Jerusalem. Messengers would then be sent to the people living throughout the region to announce that the new month had been officially declared. In the case of holidays that last only one night and day, it was important to have this information in a timely manner. If the news was delayed, Jews would often celebrate a particular holiday (Passover and Rosh

Hashanah, for example) for *two* nights, one of which was sure to be the proper night.

Now that we have improved calendar systems and communications, some Jews today celebrate certain holidays for one night only (such as Reform Jews and many Jews in Israel), while others maintain the older custom of celebrating the holiday for two nights.

A note about what constitutes a "day": in Judaism, a day begins at sundown. Why? In Genesis 1:2–5 we are told that first there was darkness and then there was light, and this is described as the first day. Since darkness (evening) came first, this is when the day begins. This is also when Shabbat begins—in the evening. As the seasons change and the time of sundown varies, the start of Shabbat (as well as every other day) varies as well. The Jewish week does not begin on Sunday or Monday; it begins at the conclusion of Shabbat—sundown (or nightfall) on Saturday evening. Observant Jews begin their Sabbath a few minutes before the sun sets; others begin at a time more convenient for the family gathering. All Jewish holidays and festivals, like Shabbat, begin in the evening and use the word *erev* to describe this. Thus Sabbath eve is referred to as Erev Shabbat.

One year we invited to Passover seder some guests who do not generally observe Jewish holidays. Their calendars indicated that the first "day" of Passover was on Thursday of that week. To their dismay, they almost missed the dinner; they did not realize that while Thursday was indeed the first "day" of Passover, the holiday actually commenced Wednesday evening.

Now that you have an idea of how the Jewish calendar operates, let's look at the Jewish holidays and festivals.

Were you to take a small survey of the non–Jewish American population, asking people to name as many Jewish holidays as they could, which ones would they mention? Probably Hanukkah, since it has become so closely associated with Christmas in an effort not to leave Jews out of the picture during the holiday (and shopping) season. Passover might also be mentioned since it, too, falls near a Christian holiday, Easter, and generates a fair amount of newspaper publicity (mostly about food!).

Perhaps non-Jews have heard of the Jewish New Year (Rosh Hashanah) or the Day of Atonement (Yom Kippur), but that may be pushing it. A lot depends on how many Jewish friends and acquaintances people have, how observant and communicative they are about their lifestyles, and what they see on television, in films, or in the newspapers.

I'm going to touch on descriptions of the principle holidays and festivals and give you a taste of what each one is about. Don't be surprised if you wind up learning some facts or details that your Jewish friends may not know.

Shabbat—The Sabbath

Early in my career, I worked in a clinic with a doctor who was an Orthodox Jew. As a result of this friendship, I began to learn a lot about Judaism. Many years later, I still vividly remember a special evening.

My colleague had invited me to his home for Shabbat (Sabbath) dinner. Although I worked with this man, felt very comfortable with him, had wonderful conversations with him, and would occasionally have lunch with him (only if I brought my own lunch, since he was strictly kosher and would not eat in the neighborhood restaurants), I still felt nervous about the upcoming Friday night dinner. I accepted the invitation, however, because I wanted to experience a contemporary Orthodox Jewish Shabbat.

On the way to his home on Friday, he bought some flowers; I got the impression that he did this on a regular basis because the florist had his order ready. I had brought some kosher wine, figuring this was a safe bet.

His wife opened the door, and I was surprised to see her very dressed up—had I not known better, I would have thought we were going out to dinner and the theater. She and I chatted while my friend changed into a three-piece suit and a dark fedora hat (which he wore throughout dinner). He explained that Shabbat is thought of as a queen, and if you are welcoming a queen to your home, wouldn't you wear your best clothes, have the house as clean as possible, be on your best behavior, and so on? I couldn't argue with that, having entertained royalty in my apartment on numerous occasions.

At a specifically determined time (just before sundown and before the official start of Shabbat), my friend's wife lit the Sabbath candles, covering her eyes while reciting the blessing. Why did she cover her eyes? Generally, a blessing is recited *before* an action takes place; for example, a blessing over food is said before eating. However, the Shabbat blessing indicates that the Sabbath has begun. Once the Sabbath has commenced, an observant Jew is not permitted to light a flame. Thus, Shabbat cannot proceed in the typical order, and to compensate for this problem, the candles are lit first. Next, we cover our eyes while we say the blessing, officially starting the Sabbath. When we uncover our eyes . . . voilà! It's officially Shabbat, and the candles are lit.

We sang some happy songs in Hebrew (I hummed along) and recited several prayers and blessings (I knew some of the basic ones, including the blessings over wine and the special Sabbath bread, known as *challah*). We then ate a great, multicourse meal. My friend and his wife were very attentive to their young son, about five years old, who was also dressed in a suit and tie. They were generous in answering my questions and were very gracious, even when I accidentally cracked one of their crystal goblets. After the meal we joined in more songs and more prayer.

My friend and his family would visit the synagogue the next day (he never worked on the Sabbath—a violation of one of the Ten Commandments as written in the Torah and delivered by God to Moses). They would walk to the synagogue, since starting the ignition of the car would amount to striking a flame. His wife would not light the stove or cook, since lighting a match or turning on electrical appliances are also forbidden on the Sabbath. In the customary manner, she had the next day's meals prepared in advance. If the phone rang (it would certainly not be one of their Orthodox friends calling), the answering machine (one of the first I'd ever seen) would pick up. The entire day would be spent in family and religious activities.

After sunset on Saturday night, they would say good-bye to the Queen Sabbath with prayer and song and with a very special havdalah ceremony. The word *havdalah* means "separation" in Hebrew. There are three special symbols for this ceremony: a goblet filled with wine, a special container of sweet-smelling spices, and a braided candle that has multiple wicks (at one end of the candle). As prayers are sung, a person tastes the wine, smells the spices, and, holding a hand near the flames of the candle, observes the reflections against his or her fingernails. Each action is symbolic of the beauty of the Sabbath and our bittersweet sadness at its departure.

Leaving the Shabbat dinner, I was elated but at the same time slightly envious. How wonderful to have such a special day to share with family, close friends, and God.

The degree to which each of us observes our God and our faith is a personal thing. But when I think of what Shabbat should be—what it could be—I always remember the evening I spent at the home of my friend and his family.

We are told in the Bible, "Remember the Sabbath day, and keep it holy. Six days you shall labor and do all your work. But the seventh day is a Sabbath to the LORD your God; you shall not do any work" (Exodus 20:8–10) and "Observe the Sabbath day and keep it holy, as the LORD your God commanded you" (Deuteronomy 5:12).

The majority of American Jews, like most Americans, do not spend the Sabbath in prayer or in the synagogue. Many work, drive, answer the phone, cook, and perform all the tasks and jobs they do every other day of the year. However, I know many Jewish people who, even though they don't consider themselves particularly religious, nevertheless remember the Sabbath in some small way special to themselves, perhaps by lighting Shabbat candles (a custom dating back at least two thousand years), attending occasional Friday night or Saturday morning services, or just avoiding certain activities in order to spend time alone or with family.

In some ways and to some people, the other six days of the week are in essence a preparation for Shabbat, in much the same way that many Americans work and save for an annual one- or two-week vacation. In truth, Shabbat *is* like a vacation—it's an opportunity to get away from the normal work and household activities that keep us occupied.

In Hebrew, the only day of the week that has its own name is Shabbat. The other days are simply numbered according to their relation to Shabbat. It is interesting to note that the Jewish Sabbath actually lasts twenty-five hours, not twenty-four. It begins eighteen minutes before sunset on Friday with the lighting of the candles, and it ends with the havdalah ceremony forty-two minutes after sunset on Saturday.

To Jews who observe Shabbat, it is a period during which they are released from the stress and drudgery of everyday tasks and are free to enjoy tranquility and spiritual reflection.

For some Jews, preparation for Shabbat may include a visit to a *mikvah,* the ritual bath. There are separate baths for men and women, and the details of the bath dimensions, water temperature, plumbing configurations, and other such minutiae are described in historical religious texts. (For an observant Jewish woman, the mikvah is also visited as a requisite step after completion of the menstrual cycle and before the woman resumes sexual relations with her husband. This is a religious and spiritual immersion, not a physical cleansing as such. In some ways, the visit to the mikvah also serves as a venue for relaxation and conversation.) Typically, the mikvah is used more often by Orthodox Jews. I have yet to visit a mikvah, but someday may get my chance.

Setting aside a day of rest is difficult. We are surrounded by too many things to do, too many places to go, and far too many distractions. What would it be like if we could ignore these distractions and spend an entire day every week with our family, our friends, and our spiritual thoughts? An answer to this hypothetical question appears in the Talmud, which tells us that the world would be redeemed if everyone observed only two consecutive Sabbaths.

The High Holidays—Rosh Hashanah and Yom Kippur

Rosh Hashanah

Rosh Hashanah begins a period known as the Ten Days of Repentance, or the Days of Awe. This period culminates with the holiday of Yom Kippur.

These ten days, which generally fall in September, are extremely important in Jewish religious life. It is the time when, it is said, God judges each of us based on our actions during the prior year. It is also the time when God decides who will live and who will die; who will be rich and who will be poor; who will be happy and who will not.

On Rosh Hashanah, the decision is written in the "Book of Life." On Yom Kippur, the book is sealed. During the ten days between these two holidays, we have an opportunity to repent and ask God's forgiveness for our sins.

Thus, you can see the importance of these holidays in the Jewish tradition and why they are called the Days of Repentance or the Days of Awe. You can also understand why many Jews who never set foot in a synagogue any other time of the year go out of their way to attend religious services during these two holidays. Because of this, special seating arrangements are often necessary, and it is not uncommon for smaller synagogues to have services in larger halls, theaters, or even churches to accommodate the many hundreds and sometimes thousands of people who wish to attend during the High Holidays. (Many High Holiday services I've attended over the years have been held in churches of various denominations.)

Rosh Hashanah is considered the Jewish New Year, but in the Jewish calendar it falls at the beginning of the seventh month. The first month of the Jewish calendar actually occurs in the spring. So how can Rosh Hashanah be the Jewish New Year? Easy (there's always an explanation for these things).

Spring marks the beginning of the civil calendar when, historically, certain crops were harvested, and it coincides with the holiday of Passover. During the High Holidays in the fall, we mark the beginning of the *religious* year. There are actually other harvests and events that are considered types of "new years." (In a similar manner, many Americans feel that the year "begins" on the first day of school in the fall. I have a friend who is a true baseball fanatic; the year begins for him on the first day of spring training.)

In the synagogue, several changes are made for the Jewish New Year. Special white coverings are placed on the ark and the lecterns, and the rabbi and cantor wear white instead of their traditional black gowns (because white is associated with purity). Many congregants wear white as well.

Another custom common to this holiday is the centuries-old ceremony called *tashlich*, which means "casting off." At an appropriate point during the first day of Rosh Hashanah (the second day if the first day falls on Shabbat), people meet near a body of water. There, after reciting certain verses, they empty their pockets (generally filled with bread crumbs) into the water, thereby symbolically "emptying their sins" as well. This is one of those ceremonies steeped in tradition and possibly superstition as well. The custom is based on the words of the prophet Micah: "You will cast all our sins into the depths of the sea" (Micah 7:19).

Tashlich is usually a fun part of the celebration. At the last tashlich service I attended, we joined three rabbis, two cantors, and a group of about sixty adults and children as we cast our sins (pieces of bread) into a nearby lake. The sins were quickly confiscated by ducks and fish.

As I mentioned previously, in earlier times when the actual day of the new moon (and therefore, the new month) was difficult to pinpoint (it could be a cloudy night, for example), it became the custom to celebrate holidays such as Rosh Hashanah on two nights. This way, people living in the outlying regions were sure to observe the proper night of the holiday on at least one of the nights. Most Jews maintain the custom of celebrating Rosh Hashanah for two nights, while some observe the holiday for one night only.

Besides celebrating the new year, Rosh Hashanah commemorates other events, too. Some Jews look to Rosh Hashanah as the anniversary of the creation of the world as well as the creation of Adam and Eve.

The Torah readings for Rosh Hashanah services include two very interesting sections. The first involves the birth of Isaac, Abraham's banishment of Hagar and Ishmael, and the subsequent rescue of the mother and child in the wilderness. The second section tells the story of the binding of Isaac, wherein Abraham's faith in God is tested when he is asked to sacrifice his son. These sections of the Torah never fail to stimulate controversy, dialogue, and inspired sermons.

The High Holidays are marked with the blowing of the shofar, a wind instrument made from the horn of a ram. The Torah (Numbers 29:1) calls for the blowing of the shofar on Rosh Hashanah: "On the first day of the seventh month you shall have a holy convocation; . . . It is a day for you to blow the trumpets." Because it is commanded that the shofar be blown, Jews have an associated obligation to *hear* it blown.

The sounds of the shofar have great historical significance. The shofar was blown when Moses received the Law on Mount Sinai:

> On the morning of the third day there was thunder and
> lightning, as well as a thick cloud on the mountain, and
> a blast of a trumpet so loud that all the people who were
> in the camp trembled. (Exodus 19:16)

The horn was blown in the original temple in Jerusalem. It was also used in times of war in much the same way as a bugle is blown during a battle. Here is an example from Joshua:

> When they make a long blast with the ram's horn, as
> soon as you hear the sound of the trumpet, then all the
> people shall shout with a great shout; and the wall of

the city will fall down flat, and all the people shall charge straight ahead. (Joshua 6:5)

In earlier times, the shofar was used as a musical instrument, and more recently it was sounded after the 1967 Six-Day War in Israel.

In traditional synagogues, the shofar is not sounded on the Sabbath. In those congregations, however, Rosh Hashanah is observed for two days, so the shofar is sounded on the second day of the holiday. The prohibition against blowing the shofar on the Sabbath does not originate in the sounding of the horn itself but in the prohibition of carrying the horn—observant Jews do not believe things should be carried on Shabbat because this is considered work, which is forbidden.

Many Jewish people send Jewish New Year's greeting cards on Rosh Hashanah, wishing that their friends and family members "Be inscribed in the Book of Life and have a good year." This period is also a time when we ask forgiveness of our family, friends, and acquaintances for any wrongs (intentional or unintentional) we may have committed against them. It is important to note, however, that asking forgiveness is not a once-a-year occasion for Jews. In fact, there is a prayer of supplication called *Tachanun* that is recited during daily prayers (on most days). This penitential prayer (the translation of the first word of the prayer means "I am guilty") teaches us that reparation can begin only when a person accepts the blame on him- or herself.

I've always felt that it may be more appropriate for a non-Jewish person to send Jewish friends a Jewish New Year's card instead of a Christmas card or even a Hanukkah card. This might show an awareness of the Jewish person's beliefs, and it marks the occasion of a significant Jewish holiday.

As with many holidays, Rosh Hashanah has traditional foods associated with it. We celebrate with a special round challah (egg bread), which is symbolic of the yearly cycle; the bread is often sweetened with raisins. Since we all wish for the new year to begin "sweetly," we dip apple sections in honey, thank God for creating the fruit of the trees, and pray for a good and sweet year. If you've never had apples dipped in honey, try it, at least once a year.

The days between the two High Holidays, the Ten Days of Repentance, are considered a period for introspection, and some Jews take this time to create what is known as an "ethical will," a document that states the person's values, hopes, insights, and beliefs. This type of document dates back to biblical times.

Yom Kippur

The Ten Days of Repentance culminate in Yom Kippur, the Day of Atonement. It is considered the most solemn day of the Jewish year, the day on which your fate is sealed.

While Yom Kippur is often referred to as the "holiest day of the year," always remember that Shabbat, the Sabbath, is truly the most significant day.

Yom Kippur is a day on which "you shall deny yourselves" (Leviticus 23:27, 32). These words have been interpreted to include a ban on eating, drinking, bathing, sex, and the wearing of leather shoes. Most Jews who are older than thirteen fast on Yom Kippur, and men who otherwise shave every day may show up at religious services looking rather grubby.

Why shouldn't we wear leather shoes? Since leather shoes were considered a luxury in ancient times, it has become a custom for some people to wear tennis shoes to the synagogue. It is not uncommon these days to see men walking to services incongruously dressed in a business suit, dress shirt and tie, and running shoes. The irony is that leather shoes were banned centuries ago because they were considered more comfortable than sandals or bare feet, and today's most comfortable shoes are probably athletic shoes, which we now wear instead of leather ones (just another example of how traditions and customs evolve and sometimes conflict).

It is traditional for Jews to fast for twenty-five hours, the same length as Shabbat (see "Shabbat—The Sabbath"), and to abstain from work. People who will never fast at any other time of the year do so on Yom Kippur, even those who do not consider themselves particularly religious. Children and people who are ill are not required to fast, although they may choose a symbolic modified fast in which certain items are omitted from their diet. Pregnant or nursing women may or may not fast depending on their beliefs and/or medical advice. Ultimately, the fast is one step toward asking forgiveness for our sins, and it helps us focus on the solemnity and significance of the holiday.

Since a day in the Jewish religion begins at sundown and ends at the following sundown, the Yom Kippur holiday begins with a special evening service called *Kol Nidre*. The Kol Nidre prayer, chanted just before sunset, is a prayer through which a person is released from promises or vows made that he or she cannot fulfill. This release, however, is meant for vows made to God and does not nullify promises made to other people. As with Rosh

Hashanah, this is a time to ask forgiveness from friends and relatives for any wrongdoing, committed knowingly or unknowingly, against another person.

The Kol Nidre prayer is sung (in the original Aramaic) to a hauntingly beautiful melody, and in many non-Orthodox congregations it is performed, often by a cellist, as a preface to the service.

The next twenty-five hours are spent fasting, in introspection, and involved in the synagogue service. Certain prayers concern the confession of sins that we may have committed against God and other people. There is also a memorial prayer for those who have died. Some congregants remove their shoes during the service as a sign of humility.

During the service, we read from the Book of Jonah, the theme of which is repentance and salvation. (After spending a few days and nights in the belly of "a great fish," you would be ready to repent, too.)

Often there is a section of the service during which the lives and tribulations of Jewish martyrs are described. I am brought to tears every year during this service as I listen to the simple but heartrending stories of my people who perished while attempting to practice their faith or merely for being Jews.

At the conclusion of the Yom Kippur service, we implore God not only to write us in the Book of Life, but to *seal* us in the Book of Life as well. One long blast from the shofar concludes the day of prayer, atonement, and fasting. Congregants like to hear a really long blast, and this is an opportunity for the shofar blower to demonstrate his or her chops.

At this point there may be a short ceremony (havdalah) to mark the end of the holiday. The customs for this ceremony vary from congregation to congregation.

It is traditional to break the fast with friends and family or with other members of the congregation. Anyone who has fasted knows that your awareness following the fast is heightened and that food eaten after a fast takes on special meaning.

If you have a trace of Jewish feeling in your bones, you know it on Yom Kippur, even if you're not particularly religious at any other time. One of my favorite stories involves Sandy Koufax, the extraordinary Dodger Hall of Fame pitcher, who refused to pitch in a World Series game on Yom Kippur. Symbolic behavior of this sort makes many Jewish people proud. I would love to see more gestures like this, not because it sets the person up as a religious icon, but because it makes the general population aware of the significance and holiness of this very special Jewish holiday.

Sukkot

Did your ancestors live and wander in the desert for forty years? Mine did. I'm reminded of it every year during the holiday of *Sukkot*.

Sukkot is a biblical holiday commemorating the forty years that the Israelites wandered in the desert, living in portable dwellings and waiting to enter the Promised Land. Sukkot falls on the fifth day after Yom Kippur and lasts for seven or eight days.

The Book of Leviticus tells us, "You shall live in booths for seven days; . . . so that your generations may know that I made the people of Israel live in booths when I brought them out of the land of Egypt" (Leviticus 23:42–43).

It is interesting to note that Sukkot occurs in the fall, not in the spring, which is when the Exodus took place. This is when the Torah tells us to celebrate it. We can second-guess why until the camels come home, but this is when we celebrate it. For centuries, Sukkot commemorated the fall harvest and anticipated the winter rainy season, which was necessary for a successful spring crop. Some observers consider Sukkot a celebration of the agricultural harvest as much as, or even more than, a remembrance of the wanderings in the wilderness.

The sukkah (booth or hut) itself is supposed to be constructed in a certain manner, but I have seen all types of structures over the years. Some were marvels of engineering skill, while others were excellent examples of how to build things using kite string.

Tradition tells us that the first nail should be driven into the sukkah as Yom Kippur ends—even before the fast is broken. The walls are supposed to be able to withstand a normal wind, and the stars should be visible through the roof. Branches, straw, bamboo, cornstalks, palm fronds, or wooden slats are often used for the roof (why am I somehow reminded of "The Three Little Pigs"?), and these materials are really what qualifies the structure as temporary.

Most of the booths I have seen do not have four walls at all. Rather, they are built to support a roof that provides shade but through which you can see the stars. From the walls and roof of the sukkah people hang leaves, dried gourds, certain fruits, and other symbols of the harvest. Pictures, posters, cards, and all kinds of imaginative items are used to decorate the structure.

Theoretically, the sukkah serves as home for the duration of the holiday. One family might eat its meals in a backyard sukkah and sleep in it as well, while another family may eat in the sukkah but sleep indoors. It all depends on how observant a family chooses to be and the accommodations that are available (and the weather).

Synagogue congregations generally build a sukkah so that everyone, especially the children, can catch the spirit of the holiday. A sukkah may be large or small, depending on the number of people it must accommodate—a family of four or a classroom of kids.

Second only to the sukkah itself are the other symbols of the holiday, including four species of plants: the citron *(etrog)*, the date palm *(lulav)*, the branch of the myrtle bush *(hadassim)*, and the branch of the willow *(avarot)*. These are referred to in Leviticus 23:40, respectively, as "The fruit of majestic *(hada)* trees, branches of palm trees, boughs of leafy trees, and willows of the brook." Blessings are recited while the branches of these four species, arranged in a specific manner, are held and waved in various directions. East, north, west, south, then up toward heaven and down toward the earth. We wave the branches in all these directions as a reminder that God is everywhere and as a ritual request to God for sufficient rainfall.

In the synagogue, a special prayer is made while congregants carry the "four species" in a procession around the Torah. On the seventh and last day of Sukkot a special service for rain is held, a reminder of our agricultural traditions.

Because of its direct connection to the earth, crops and the elements, Sukkot provides a wonderful opportunity to reflect on our relationship to our planet and the important role each of us plays in helping to protect it.

Simchat Torah

The reading of the Torah portion each week in the synagogue is arranged in such a way that in a year's time the entire Torah scroll can be read. (Some congregations choose to read a third of each portion instead, thus completing the entire Torah in a three-year cycle.)

Simchat Torah means "rejoicing of the Torah (the Law)." This joyous celebration takes place on the last day of Sukkot and marks the day we read the final verses of Deuteronomy—the last of the Five Books of Moses. However, we don't miss a beat. We complete the circle of Torah study by reading the first verses of Genesis the same day.

Reading the Torah is an ongoing process, and this process of ending and then beginning once again is celebrated with singing, waving little flags, and dancing with the Torah. Some liken it to the joy of a Jewish wedding celebration, and let me tell you, it's a fun party.

We begin the observance of Simchat Torah with the lighting of candles and traditional blessings for wine and bread, as well as with a special prayer for the season. Parents bring their children to the synagogue, where all of the Torah scrolls are removed from the ark and paraded around the room by men, women, and children, often in winding patterns and circles. In many non-Orthodox synagogues, the singing may be accompanied by guitars and other instruments. It is an honor to carry the Torah during this happy celebration, and typically just about everyone gets a chance to participate. In some neighborhoods, the dancing, singing, and parading spill into the streets.

So, if some night you pass a synagogue and dozens of revelers are singing and dancing while carrying Hebrew scrolls above their heads, you can be pretty sure it's Simchat Torah!

Hanukkah—Is It Really the "Jewish Christmas"?

When I ask a non-Jewish person, "What is Hanukkah? What do you know about it?" I generally receive answers that describe it as "A time when Jewish kids get lots of presents" or "The holiday when Jews light candles" or, my favorite, "It's the Jewish Christmas."

Considering what the holiday has become in American society, these descriptions are not far from wrong. As a matter of fact, it is the general perception of Hanukkah that prompted me to write this book in the first place.

Hanukkah commemorates two events. First, there was a great battle (circa 165 BCE) in which the Maccabees and their family, the Hasmoneans, were victorious over Antiochus Epiphanes. Antiochus, the king of the Syrian Greek empire, had forbidden the Jewish people from practicing their religion and had forced pagan rituals on them. The temple in Jerusalem had been defiled, idols had been installed, and it had thus been made unfit for Jewish religious purposes. It was an ugly scene.

After the Maccabees' military victory, it was necessary to rebuild, cleanse, and reconsecrate the temple altar. As part of the rededication in 164 BCE, it was necessary to relight the temple menorah (the seven-branched candelabra, also known as a *hanukkiah*), but as a result of the desecration of the temple (and according to legend), only one jar of holy oil—enough to kindle the light for one day—remained. A miracle occurred, though, and the light burned for eight days.

So, there you have the two principle reasons for the Hanukkah festival—the Maccabees' military victory over tyranny and the rededication of the temple (and the related miracle of the oil). Some scholars propose that the story of the miracle was introduced into the holiday season by the Rabbis (see "The Torah and the Law"), who preferred not to emphasize the military aspect of the celebration or to imitate the paganlike candle-lighting solstice celebrations that generally occurred at this dark time of the year.

To celebrate the eight days of the miracle, each night we light a candle in a special Hanukkah candelabra, a menorah, as we recite or sing a prayer. The first night, we light one candle (using a *shammes*, or "servant" candle); the second night, we light two candles, and so on, until the last night of the holiday when we have a total of eight candles (plus the shammes). Some families have more than one menorah, maybe one for each child or family guest. It is a custom to display the menorah in the window for everyone to see.

On Shabbat it is customary to light the Hanukkah candles *before* the Sabbath candles.

Now that you know the origin of the Hanukkah holiday and have lit the menorah, let's eat!

The traditional holiday foods use a lot of oil (get it?). According to the customs of the various Jewish communities, we eat potato latkes (pancakes) fried in oil or doughnuts (also fried in oil). Jelly doughnuts, known as *sufganiyot*, are a big treat in many homes, especially in Israel. Recipes for latkes abound. My mother's are the best.

A word about gambling: Judaism is traditionally against gambling (according to the Talmud and other Jewish historical writings). There is a lifting of the rules at Hanukkah time, however, and it is common on this holiday for children and adults to play a game with a four-sided top called a dreidel. The stakes are usually pennies, chocolate coins, or other similar items (we recently used peanuts in the shell). Everyone antes up, and someone spins the dreidel. You win, lose, put more into the ante, or stay even, depending on which side turns up.

Up until the State of Israel was established, the letters on the dreidel symbolized the words, "A great miracle happened *there.*" In Israel, the dreidel is designed with symbols that represent the statement, "A great miracle happened *here.*" Thus, with the creation of Israel in 1948, the whole dreidel industry was turned upside down (actually, on its side).

Hanukkah gelt (money) is small amounts of money given to children by the family. However, the giving of gifts has acquired greater and greater emphasis, and that's what most people associate with the holiday of Hanukkah today. For better or worse, Hanukkah, a minor, nonreligious festival, has become the religious occasion observed by more American Jews than any other.

Christmas and Hanukkah, however, are quite different holidays.

Christmas celebrates the birth of Jesus (although the exact date of birth is unknown, this was the date set aside to celebrate the day of Jesus' birth). Many Christians, who view Christmas primarily as a religious holiday, will attend Mass as part of their Christmas celebration. Even though nonchurchgoers may be in the Christmas spirit, the holiday is still founded on a major religious event.

Hanukkah, on the other hand, is a postbiblical holiday and therefore does not carry the importance of biblical holidays such as Passover, Rosh Hashanah, and Yom Kippur. There are no restrictions on secular activities during Hanukkah: Jewish kids don't stay home from school, and Jewish adults don't stay home from work. Synagogue activities during Hanukkah revolve around playing games and organizing latke parties.

Then again, we can't deny that many, if not most, people who celebrate Christmas view the period within the framework of the "holiday season." It is a time for gift giving, charity, good cheer, music, parties, trees, lights, elves, and Santa!

Is it a "conflict of interest" for a Jew to give a Christian a Christmas gift? Of course not! And what about a case when someone gives a Jewish friend a Christmas present? Must we call it a Hanukkah present? I'm not sure. Maybe we should just call it a gift.

I am reminded of an advertising campaign years ago for Levy's "Jewish" rye bread that featured smiling Asians, African Americans, and people of other ethnicities and races each eating a slice of rye bread; the caption read, "You don't have to be Jewish to love Levy's."

Well, you don't have to be Christian to enjoy the spirit of Christmas, to give a gift or send a card to a friend or business associate. All you're doing is showing respect, care, and love on the occasion of your friend's holiday. The whole business of sending Christmas cards and/or Hanukkah cards is a confusing one. On the one hand, I am not offended if I receive a Christmas card. On the other hand, I am often pleasantly shocked when I receive a Hanukkah card from a Gentile friend. (I also spoke about greeting cards in the section on the Jewish New Year.)

At Christmas, I, like many American Jews, become immersed in the spirit of the holiday season and emerge from this dimension on December 26. Talk to many Jews about what they feel during "the Christmas season," and you will be surprised by the response. Some may feel alienated, others envious, and others isolated. From my own personal experience, I can say that answering someone's innocent question, "How did *you* celebrate Christmas?" has never been simple.

I suggest, however, that the two holidays, Hanukkah and Christmas, are now inseparably linked in America. I vividly recall a photograph of a previous president of the United States entertaining a group of Jewish schoolchildren as they played a game of dreidel in the Oval Office during Hanukkah. It was a wonderful shot of the kids playing, the cantor smiling, and the president showing undivided attention to the children. Very prominent in the photo's background was a large Christmas tree.

Purim

The holiday of *Purim* has all the aspects of a fairy tale—a great king, a wicked prime minister, a beautiful young queen (who has a secret), a plot to kill the king, a turn of events, vindication of those condemned to death, the execution of the villain, and a great celebration feast. Who could ask for more? Let me tell you the story (commemorated in the Book of Esther).

The action takes place in the ancient walled city of Shushan (the biblical Susa) in Persia. King Ahasuerus (Xerxes) has just had his queen, Vashti, banished for disobedience (this sets up tension since our heroine will also disobey, thus risking her own head). Following a search for the most beautiful virgins in the land, Esther (in secret, a Jewish woman) is chosen to be queen.

Esther has been raised by her cousin Mordecai. At one point, Mordecai overhears a plot by two guards to assassinate the king. Mordecai gives this information to Esther who passes it on to the king, who thwarts the plot but neglects to reward Mordecai (the king was too busy; maybe he was in the harem).

Around this time, the king appoints a man named Haman to be his second in command. Haman demands that all bow down before him, but Mordecai refuses. As a penalty, Haman plots the death not only of Mordecai but of all the Jews in the kingdom, the killing to be done on a single day. Haman convinces the king that this would be a good idea, and Haman casts lots to determine which day will be the day of execution (the word *Purim* derives from the word for "lot").

When Mordecai hears of the plan to murder the Jews, he is despondent; he tears his clothes and he dresses in sackcloth and ashes. In the provinces, as the word spreads, other Jews do the same. Esther has a servant question Mordecai about his behavior and wardrobe and she is told of Haman's plot. Mordecai reminds Esther that she, too, is at risk and that she may be in a royal position for a higher purpose than just to be a queen.

Risking her life, Esther fasts and then approaches the king, inviting him and Haman to a special dinner. Meanwhile, Haman, at the suggestion of his wife and friends, orders the gallows to be built.

On a sleepless night sometime before the dinner party, the king requests to have the royal history read to him and is reminded of Mordecai's good deed regarding the assassination plot and the fact that no reward was given. The king asks Haman what he recommends should be done for a person whom the king wishes to honor. Believing that he himself is the one to be honored, Haman responds that the person should be dressed in the king's clothes and crown, and then paraded through the city on the king's horse, with someone crying out, "Thus shall be done for the person the king wishes to honor."

Haman is dealt a blow when he is chosen to be the crier while leading Mordecai, astride a horse and wearing magnificent clothes, through the city. After being told what happened, Haman's wife predicts his downfall.

Later, at the dinner party, Queen Esther reveals her true identity as a Jew. The king turns on Haman and not only saves the Jews of the city but also condemns Haman to the noose once meant for Mordecai. Mordecai is made the chief minister, and the king and queen live happily ever after.

(Note: The aftermath of the story contains additional deaths, hangings, and many violent scenes inappropriate for a family-oriented book such as this one.)

The story of Purim, which might be based on Persian legend, does not occur in the original Five Books of Moses (the Torah) and is therefore considered a minor holiday. It is recorded in the Book of Esther, originally transcribed on a scroll. In the synagogue, the story is still read from a scroll known as a *megillah*, and that's where the expression "the whole megillah" comes from. Whenever Haman's name is read during the service, it is traditional to stomp your feet and clap your hands and use noise-makers, a custom derived from a biblical command to blot out the name of the tyrant Amalek, who is believed to be an ancestor of Haman.

Other traditions of the holiday, which usually falls in March, include giving gifts of money to the poor, sending gifts of food to friends, feasting, and having one (or many!) drinks in celebration. Everyone has a lot of fun on Purim, including the rabbi.

It is a time for laughter, jokes, and *not* taking oneself seriously. Sermons range from the ridiculous to the absurd, synagogue newsletters and magazines contain outrageous narratives, and craziness abounds.

Typical forms of revelry during Purim include parades, parties, the wearing of costumes, and reenactments of the story. More than one rabbi, portraying Queen Esther, dresses in drag for the occasion (since cross-dressing is strictly forbidden in Judaism, believe me when I say that a lot of rules are lifted, bent, and tossed out the window on this holiday).

I remember one Purim play I participated in as a child. My mother (a very clever woman) designed a costume that enabled me, dressed as Mordecai, to make an on-stage rags-to-riches transformation simply by turning the robe inside out. This was during the pre-Velcro era.

Finally, as always, there's the food. A holiday meal is traditionally served in the afternoon, and the featured delicacies are hamantaschen, little triangular pastries filled with fruit, cheese, or poppy seeds. While the word *hamantaschen* means "Haman pockets," many of us think of the pastries as little three-cornered hats, just like the one Haman might have worn. Hamantaschen taste great—try some.

One more note: Most scholars agree that the Purim story is pure fiction—none of it took place at all. Personally, I couldn't say one way or the other.

Passover

Passover is a wonderful Jewish holiday. Before and after the festive Passover seder meal, we recount the history of the slavery of the Jews in Egypt, recall the ten plagues, and hear the story of the Exodus—God's deliverance of the Jewish people. We eat unleavened bread called *matzo*, a reminder that the escaping slaves did not have time to wait for their bread to rise before baking it. We also recite the Four Questions ("Why is this night different from all other nights?"), learn about the Four Sons, and observe children at our seder searching for a piece of matzo known as the *afikomen* (the hunt ends with the payment of a reward or "ransom" to the child who finds the hidden treasure).

Along with all the gaiety, there are somber notes during the evening; we are remembering our ancestors who were slaves. It is not uncommon at some point during the evening to recall other times when we, as Jews, were persecuted and enslaved and to remember the millions who perished at the hands of our oppressors in more recent history. Finally, when we reflect on the plagues visited on the enemies of the Israelites, including the visitation of the angel of death on the firstborn, we can begin to sense the powerful message of Passover.

The degree to which members of a family prepare for the holiday depends on how religious and observant they are. It is important to remember that in the United States there are all levels of Jewish observance. One family may follow the traditions in a strict manner—changing dishware before the holiday, eating only permitted foods, and following the ritual to the letter. Another family might get together with extended family members and friends, have a casual Passover meal, and that's it. Like all family and religious rituals, the more you put into Passover, the more you get out of it.

Passover, known in Hebrew as *Pesach*, is a biblical holiday and occurs in the spring. It is observed for seven or eight days and is marked by a major (and demanding) change in diet. The Bible and the Talmud tell us that any product that is leavened or fermented may not be consumed during the holiday (this includes bread, cake, cookies, beer, liquor, and so forth). In addition, any food product that is likely to ferment is excluded (including pastas, many types of cereals, and products made from flour). Ashkenazic Jews avoid eating rice as well as beans, peas, legumes, and corn. Sephardic Jews include rice and legumes in their Passover diet. One reason for this is that potatoes and other root vegetables were not available to substitute for bread in the regions from which they came (see "Ashkenazic and Sephardic Jews").

Some seemingly acceptable foods may contain ingredients such as cornstarch that put them in the unacceptable category. In the homes of observant Jews, the excluded products are removed from the house (or hidden) as part of a cleaning and inspection ritual.

Through the years, Jewish cooks and kosher food manufacturers have become incredibly creative in finding substitutes for forbidden ingredients; such alternative ingredients include potato starch and matzo meal. Whether you consider Passover cereal that looks like Cheerios but tastes like matzo appetizing or not is beside the point. Just remember that "kosher" and "kosher for Passover" are not the same thing; "kosher for Passover" foods do not contain any forbidden ingredients.

It is traditional to invite guests to a seder. If you receive an invitation and want to bring something, check with the hosts first, or bring fruit or Passover wine or Passover candy. While it may seem safe to bring a green salad, some ingredients are not acceptable to all observant Jews; the inclusion of sprouts in your salad may make it unacceptable to families who do not eat legumes during the holiday. Then there could be an issue about the salad bowl you bring if the family uses special Passover dishes.

In preparation for the holiday, the house is scoured and inspected for any traces of leavened products (called *hametz*), including bread, crumbs, and so on. As might be expected, specific prayers can accompany these procedures.

For many years non-Jews have had a role in this holiday. Since it would be a financial hardship (as well as a waste) for poorer Jews to rid themselves of all the "non-Passover" food and drink in their home, an arrangement was made with a non-Jewish person to symbolically purchase it all, only to have the transaction terminated (for a token sum to make it an official transaction) at the end of the holiday. This procedure was generally arranged by the community rabbi and fulfilled the biblical requirement that there be no hametz in a Jewish home during Passover.

Today, many Jewish households will temporarily replace their everyday dishes, cookware, and utensils and use only those designated for Passover. All this may sound like a lot of work and extremely elaborate, and it is. The ritual preparation of a Jewish home for Passover is one of the most stringent spring cleanings you could imagine.

We celebrate the first night of Passover with a holiday meal called the seder. (Many Jews also conduct a seder on the second night of Passover.) From beginning to end, from the first blessing over the wine to the last song and prayer, we follow the order of the seder (the word means "order" in Hebrew) as listed in a book called a *Haggadah*. This booklet contains prayers, songs, and psalms, as well as a recounting of the Exodus story.

The Haggadah of my youth was published by Maxwell House Coffee, and I have since found out that upward of 35 million of these *Haggadot* (plural) have been distributed by Maxwell House since 1934. There were advertisements of food products on some of the pages. Things are different today. Each year at Passover many bookstore displays literally overflow with Haggadot that cater to each and every sect, taste, special interest, age, lifestyle, persuasion, and amalgam of humanity. There's a Haggadah for the vegetarian seder, the seder for non-Jews, the gender-neutral/egalitarian seder, the gay and lesbian seder, the gay and lesbian Jewish/Christian/Buddhist bilingual ovo-lacto vegetarian seder, the "fifteen-minute" seder, the young Republican seder— you name it. Seders, like bagels, have become nonsectarian, and that, I suppose, is just the evolution of things. There are allegedly several thousand published versions of the Haggadah available, and more are coming all the time.

During a typical seder, one person assumes the role of leader. Family members and friends are seated around the dinner table and each has a copy of the Haggadah. Remember, most Jews do this every year, and it's as familiar as Thanksgiving dinner or a Super Bowl party.

The table is set with dishes and wineglasses, and in the center is a seder plate. On this special plate, which may be ornate or specially crafted, several symbolic food items are placed:

- a shank bone of a lamb, symbolic of the Paschal (Passover) sacrifice offered at the temple in Jerusalem in early times; it is called *zeroah* (sometimes a roasted chicken bone is used; vegetarians may use a beet or other vegetable)
- a roasted hard-boiled egg, to commemorate the festival sacrifice brought to the temple during the spring; it is called *beitzah* and is also thought to commemorate the destruction of the First and Second Temples (see "The Temple")
- a sample of bitter herbs, known as *maror,* which symbolizes the bitterness of our slavery in Egypt (horseradish is typically used)
- a sample of a vegetable, known as *karpas* (parsley, lettuce, or boiled potato are typical); later, this vegetable will be dipped in salted water and eaten
- a special mixture of nuts, fruits, cinnamon, and wine or juice, called *haroset,* which is symbolic of the

mortar used by the Jewish slaves in performing hard labor

- a second vegetable, also bitter, known as *hazeret* (romaine lettuce, watercress, radish, or cucumber are often used)

In addition, there is a plate on which there are three whole pieces of matzo, covered or placed in a cloth container. The middle piece is broken in two; one half becomes the afikomen.

The seder begins with the lighting of the holiday candles and proceeds to the prayer over the wine. Wine is symbolic of the fruit of the earth; if you don't drink alcohol or don't like wine, grape juice (also made from the "fruit of the vine") is a good substitute. Custom tells us we're supposed to drink four full cups of wine during the seder, and I'm sure many people do. But if you have to drive home after the seder, it's probably not a great idea. (The last time I can remember drinking four full glasses of wine at a seder, I was ten years old. That was a seder I'll never forget.)

The seder proceeds with a ritual washing of the hands, the dipping in saltwater and tasting of the *karpas* (saltwater reminds us of the tears Jews shed as slaves), the breaking of the middle matzo, and the hiding of the afikomen.

While lifting up the plate that holds the matzo so that everyone at the table can see it, the leader speaks the first lines of the story of Passover: "This is the bread of affliction our ancestors ate in the land of Egypt. Let all who are hungry come and eat. Let all who are needy come and celebrate the Passover with us."

Throughout the recitation of the Passover story we are reminded of our slavery before the Exodus. It is incumbent on each person at the seder to share in the telling as though he or she personally came out of Egypt.

Next is the recitation of the Four Questions, which is usually done by the youngest child at the table, who often is aided by the older kids if necessary. Sometimes the "youngest child" at a seder turns out to be an adult.

The Four Questions all relate to the principle question, "Why is this night different from all other nights?"

- On all other nights we eat either leavened or unleavened bread; why on this night do we eat only unleavened bread?
- On all other nights we eat any type of herb; why on this night do we eat only bitter herbs?
- On all other nights we do not dip our herbs even once (in saltwater); why on this night do we dip them twice?
- On all other nights we eat our meal either sitting or reclining; why on this night do we eat reclining?

For the answers to the Four Questions, I invite you to attend a seder. We often have non-Jewish friends at our seder table, and I have many Christian friends who conduct seder meals of their own.

After the Four Questions, there is a description of the Four Sons. Clearly, the number four has some significance in the holiday. (Gender roles in Judaism have changed with the times. The story of the Four Sons is replaced at many contemporary Passover meals by the story of the Four Children. My mother reminds me—with some regret—that although she was the youngest child in her family, the Four Questions were always recited by her older brother—the youngest son.)

The Four Sons is a parable that describes four different levels of belief and understanding, and it reminds us of the importance of teaching religious traditions to our children. The first son is a wise son who asks about the customs that God commands us to observe. The second son is a wicked son (some say "evil," but he's always been "wicked" to me) who does not include himself in the group but instead asks about the customs that God commanded *you* to observe. The third son is a simple son who is confused or indifferent and lacks knowledge, and the fourth son is a young or naive son who is not able even to ask the question about the importance of the commandments. It is to these very different types of children that we are obligated to tell the story of Passover and the Exodus.

Next on the Passover agenda is the telling of the story of the Exodus, Moses' recurring plea to "Let my people go," and the visitation of the ten plagues on Egypt after Pharaoh refused Moses' request. Each of the ten plagues is recited in turn as each person spills a drop of wine on his or her plate.

Here are the ten plagues, in order of visitation (along with variations according to different translations):

- the Nile waters are turned to blood;
- the country is overrun by frogs;
- there is an infestation of gnats;
- swarms of flies invade the country (or hordes of wild beasts roam wild);

- a deadly pestilence infects cattle and livestock (pestilence);
- there is an inflammation of boils on man and beast alike;
- hailstorms wreak havoc on the land;
- swarms of locusts devour the remainder of the crops;
- a thick darkness descends over the land for three days; and
- every firstborn in Egypt dies.

With the conclusion of the story, blessings over the matzo ("the bread of affliction") are made and pieces of the unleavened bread are eaten. The bitter herbs and the *haroset* (mortar mixture) are tasted. The egg, symbolizing the holiday sacrifice, is dipped in saltwater and eaten.

The Passover meal is served. It's finally time to eat!

After a wonderful dinner, the previously hidden piece of matzo, the *afikomen* (which means "dessert" in Greek), is located by a child, who receives a gift or "ransom" for finding it. Now we proceed to the conclusion of the seder.

During the service, two cups of wine have been taken, and now we drink from the third cup. We then open the door to welcome the prophet Elijah to join us. Elijah, associated in ancient legend with the coming of the messiah, has his own cup of wine set on the table.

Soon, the fourth (and final!) cup of wine is drunk, and we sing some of our favorite Passover songs. One song about a small goat kid is symbolic about the trials, tribulations, and emancipation by God of the Jewish people; another, "Go Down, Moses," is a well-known spiritual and is one of my favorites.

At the conclusion of the seder is the perennial wish that we all meet "Next year in Jerusalem." Besides expressing that it would be wonderful to see Jerusalem, especially a Jerusalem filled with *peace,* the statement expresses our desire that we might all continue to be free.

A reminder: if you've had four cups of wine, someone else should drive home.

Shavuot—The Harvest Festival

Shavuot is a holiday that celebrates the harvest. It falls in the late spring and is linked to both the holiday of Passover and the deliverance of the Ten Commandments on Mount Sinai.

The Bible tells us, "You shall observe the festival of the harvest, of the first fruits of your labor, of what you sow in the field" (Exodus 23:16). It also tells us, "You shall observe the festival of harvest, of the first fruits of your labor, of what you sow in the field. You shall observe the festival of ingathering at the end of the year, when you gather in from the field the fruit of your labor," and "when you offer a grain offering of new grain to the LORD at your festival of weeks, you shall have a holy convocation" (Numbers 28:26).

In the days of the sacred temple (see "The Temple"), Jewish pilgrims would travel to Jerusalem in the spring bringing a portion of wheat, flour, and bread made from the first cuttings of the new (spring) harvest as an offering and thanks to God.

Shavuot is Hebrew for "weeks" and refers to the fact that the holiday falls seven weeks (forty-nine days) after Passover. Beginning with the second day of Passover, people gave one measure (or *omer*) of barley per day as an offering to God. Shavuot marks the end of the Passover season and is actually celebrated on the fiftieth day after Passover, which is why the festival also is known as *Pentecost* (from the Greek word meaning "fiftieth").

Since Shavuot coincides with the giving of the Torah to the Jews, and because we have become a more urban rather than agricultural population, the holiday is more closely associated today with the Revelation on Mount Sinai than with the harvest per se.

Many customs have come to be associated with this holiday, including eating dairy products. Why? After receiving the Torah, the people did not have time to properly prepare their meat products to make them kosher according to the new Law, so they ate what was permissible and simple to prepare.

The night of Shavuot (remember that Jewish holidays start at sundown on the "day before" the holiday and end at sundown on the "day of" the holiday), more observant Jews stay up all night studying the Torah, sometimes in marathon discussion sessions, a custom dating back to the sixteenth-century mystics. In Jerusalem, many thousands of people, having studied all night, descend on the Western Wall to pray on the morning of Shavuot.

Jewish homes and synagogues are decorated with green plants and cuttings as reminders of the harvest, fruit trees, the spring, and Mount Sinai. Shavuot is also a time when many young people participate in confirmation ceremonies at their religious schools (see "Confirmation").

During Shavuot, in synagogue we read the Book of Ruth. Ruth, whose story takes place in the spring, embraced Judaism and, according to the Jewish tradition, is the model of the righteous convert. Ruth was an ancestor of King David, who (it is said) was born and died on Shavuot.

Now you know more about Shavuot than *I* ever did.

Other Religious Events

Judaism has many religious days, festivals, and holidays that some people would consider minor but that are significant in their own right for what they represent or celebrate.

Lag B'Omer **is the thirty-third day after Passover.** Forty-nine days passed between the freeing of the Israelites from slavery, marked by Passover, and the giving of the Torah to the people, marked by Shavuot (see "Shavuot—The Harvest Festival"). For many observant Jews, these forty-nine days are a time to recall the period during which the Romans persecuted the Jews; it is a time to remember and mourn the many rabbis martyred during the persecution. It is a solemn time for those who observe this period of mourning; for them there are no festivities during these days, including weddings, except for a brief respite on Lag B'Omer.

Lag B'Omer is a type of semiholiday and is given over entirely to picnics, celebrations, and (as you might imagine) quite a number of weddings that could not be held during the previous thirty-two days. It marks the thirty-third day of the counting of the *omer*, the measures of barley grain set apart as an offering at the temple.

Tu B'Shevat **is the Jewish Arbor Day.** The words mean "the fifteenth of the Hebrew month of Shvat," and Tu B'Shevat falls in or near February. The Talmud describes the holiday as the "New Year of the Trees," and, as in ancient Israel, modern Israelis, particularly schoolchildren, participate in planting trees. There are ancient rules that once determined when a new tree could be harvested and how much of the crop was to be given to the temple priests (refer to the sections "The Temple" and "Jewish Priests"). Tu B'Shevat might be linked to these customs. The holiday is often celebrated by eating fruit, planting seeds and trees, and recognizing the importance of nature and ecology. Some Jewish families mark the holiday with a seder meal, emphasizing many varieties of fresh fruit as well as wine, flowers, and other things from the garden.

Rosh Hodesh **marks the first day of each Hebrew month.** The occasion of the new moon was traditionally a time for religious ceremony and was linked to women's menstrual cycles. As a result, Rosh Hodesh was and still is viewed as a women's holiday. It is often a time when women's groups gather to study, pray, and socialize.

Yom HaShoah, **Holocaust Remembrance Day, is a time each spring when Jews remember the Holocaust.** It is a solemn day that takes on different forms in different congregations, but it generally includes the lighting of six candles, one for each million people killed, and a remembrance of the non-Jews murdered in the Holocaust (see "Anti-Semitism" and "The Holocaust").

Tisha B'Av **(which means "the ninth day of the month of Av") marks a day of mourning for the destruction of the temples in Jerusalem.** It has also become associated with other events that were destructive to the Jewish people, such as the expulsion of the Jews from England, Spain, Vienna, and elsewhere. The day is marked by fasting and observing other signs of mourning that are traditional in the Jewish faith, including the lighting of memorial candles, sitting in low chairs, and not shaving.

During Tisha B'Av, we read the Book of Lamentations at synagogue. Lamentations describes the loss of Jerusalem and the temple. Tisha B'Av is thus a holiday of mourning, grief, and remembrance of times when the Jewish people had a different way of life.

Jewish Life
Cycle Events

A Jewish Wedding

L arry and Susan are finally getting married! It is the first marriage for both, and with their permission I have invited you to their wedding.

We are fortunate because it's a beautiful Sunday afternoon, and the setting—an old lodge nestled within gardens and lawns—is lovely.

Friends and family of the bride and groom mill about. Some of the cousins, aunts, and uncles have not seen one another for a long time, and many of the family members see one another only at weddings and funerals. Introductions are made, and you meet some of the out-of-town guests. All share stories about the happy couple, and the stories family members tell give you a different perspective of the character of people you've known for only a few years.

Genesis 1:28 tells us that God said, "Be fruitful and multiply" and Genesis 2:18 says, "It is not good that the man should be alone." Thus, Judaism is definitely promarriage and in favor of procreation. As a matter of fact, it regards marriage as the ideal state.

Jewish marriages do not take place on Shabbat (the Jewish Sabbath) since they would violate the prohibition of work and travel on the Sabbath. Weddings also do not take place on the major religious holidays. It is proscribed that we not mix one *simcha* (happy or joyous occasion) with another, to ensure that both events receive our full attention (Shabbat is considered the ultimate simcha). In addition, except for a brief respite, Jewish weddings are not scheduled during the forty-nine days between the holidays of Passover and Shavuot (see "Other Religious Events"). Other than these prohibitions, the ceremony can take place on any other day of the week, during the day or in the evening.

Although according to traditional Jewish law a male must be at least thirteen years old to marry and a female twelve, rabbis and the State of Israel generally require the individuals to be at least seventeen or eighteen.

By the time of the Talmud (c. 500 CE), monogamy was the norm. (The Torah, Talmud, and other writings are described and discussed in "The Torah and the Law".) Monogamy was not required, however, until the twelfth century. Today, the law of the State of Israel forbids bigamy, but exceptions have been made, such as in the special case of the Yemeni Jews, some of whom moved to Israel with more than one wife; these men were not required to divorce wives they married before the move.

Jewish law—not *Israeli* law, which is a different thing— prohibits marriages between certain relatives. A nephew, for example, may not marry his aunt, but an uncle *is* permitted to marry his niece! A man may not marry his wife's sister as long as the wife is still alive; in Orthodox Judaism (and in Israel), a member of the priestly clan (a Kohen) is not permitted to marry a divorcee (see "Jewish Priests"). (Marrying outside the Jewish faith is an issue I'll address later in "Intermarriage.")

A Jewish wedding, like any religious wedding, combines civil and religious ceremonies; the rabbi is sanctioned by the state to perform the rite, and the union is recognized according to the Jewish religion as well.

The ceremony itself is a two-part affair. The first part of the ceremony, *kiddushin,* is the "sanctification" or betrothal (the Hebrew word kiddushin comes from the word for "holy"). The groom gives the ring to the bride in front of witnesses, and she takes it as a sign of her acceptance and acquiescence. At one time, a silver or gold coin was used.

The second stage of the wedding, *nissuin,* is the "elevation" or actual marriage ceremony (*nissuin* in Hebrew means "to lift" or "to carry"). Seven special blessings (*Sheva Brachot*) are recited during the second stage of the ceremony. This is where the groom takes the bride as his wife.

In days of old, the first part of the ceremony could be separated from the second by as long as a year. During this period, as the groom set up a home for the bride, sexual relations did not occur, and the union could be terminated only with divorce or death. Obviously, it was more than just engagement as we know it today.

Now back to *our* ceremony, which is about to begin. The wedding (or bridal) canopy, known as a *chuppah,* is often made of an embroidered cloth. Sometimes a prayer shawl, known in Hebrew as a *tallit*, is used. The cloth or tallit is attached to four poles, often held aloft by four members of the wedding party. The chuppah is a symbol of the groom's home, which the bride is entering; it can also be thought of as symbolizing the tents of the ancient Hebrews. Parents of the bride and groom may walk their children down the aisle, demonstrating a union of the families rather than the "giving away" of their son or daughter.

The musicians begin to play traditional wedding music, and the procession begins. Following the family and wedding party members, Susan joins Larry, the rabbi, and the cantor under the chuppah. Susan begins to walk slowly in a circle around Larry. In a traditional ceremony, a bride encircles the groom seven times. In today's more egalitarian ceremony, the bride first encircles the groom, then the groom encircles the bride; and finally, they encircle each other. (There are many variations of the encircling ceremony.)

The idea of the bride walking around the groom is based on several different customs, scripture verses, and superstitions. Encircling the groom is a declaration that he will be the center of her existence, or, in doing so, she may protect him from demons or enemies that may try to harm him. It is also a public acknowledgment of her acceptance of her husband. Even today, when the roles of husband and wife are far different from those in earlier times, the encircling is a special and touchingly dramatic moment in the ceremony.

The kiddushin (betrothal) takes place after the recitation of blessings. The couple drinks from the first of two cups of wine they will share. The groom places the ring on the bride's right forefinger and, with the rabbi's assistance, says in Hebrew, "You are consecrated to me according to the laws of Moses and Israel." The bride makes a similar statement as she places a ring on her husband's finger.

At this point, the rabbi reads from the *ketubbah*—the Jewish marriage decree. The ketubbah, which is often decorated with designs, paintings, or drawings and calligraphy, contains language dating back to the first century CE. Historically written in Aramaic, the ketubbah may mention information about the trousseau and the dowry; it also attests to the marriage and describes the legal obligations of the husband to the wife should he divorce her or die. (Should Larry and Susan eventually divorce, what's written in the ketubbah will be overshadowed by decisions made in civil court.) A modern ketubbah may include marriage vows that the bride and groom have written themselves.

(It is important to note that Orthodox Jewish ceremonies follow more traditional customs. Among other differences, the groom does not encircle the bride, the bride does not repeat the statement consecrating her to the husband, and typically only the groom signs the ketubbah. Jewish weddings combine traditional customs and modern innovations according to the beliefs and desires of the bride and groom, their families, and their religious community. In Israel, the ketubbah may actually include monetary "penalties" in the event of divorce.)

The couple now shares a second cup of wine, marking the second half of the ceremony. The seven blessings are recited—one over the wine and the remainder praising God and asking for the happiness of the couple in marriage.

Then comes the moment that many are waiting for. "The kiss?" Well, that's a wonderful moment, too, but I mean the moment when the groom breaks the glass with his foot. The breaking of the glass has been a source of much speculation and philosophizing. It is often said that the act serves to remind us of the destruction of the temple in Jerusalem in 70 CE. There is an ancient belief that enthusiasm—the joy of the wedding ceremony, for example—should be tempered somewhat, in this case by a thought about the temple's destruction (see "The Temple").

Often, the fragile nature of the glass is compared with the fragility of a relationship, a reminder that we must treat one another with loving care. Some people believe it represents a breaking of the ties with parents as the couple begins a new life together.

In the Middle Ages it was common for the groom to take the wineglass from which he and the bride had just drunk and smash it against the north wall—the direction from which it was believed that evil spirits and enemies came. The noise acted as a deterrent to these demons. Even today, many cultures believe that noise wards off evil spirits—the ringing of church bells and whistling while passing a cemetery are remnants of this belief.

So, if there happen to be any evil spirits, demons, or enemies lurking, Larry has warded them off by stomping on a glass wrapped in a cloth napkin.

(Often a light bulb is substituted for the glass. A friend of mine insisted on using a wineglass at his wedding. Glass shards broke through the sole of his shoe, and he left the wedding canopy trailing blood. He strongly recommends using the light bulb, although many grooms continue to use a glass.)

As Larry stomps on the glass, guests cry *Mazel tov!* and *Siman tov!* The phrases mean "good luck" and "good omen," respectively, and you'll hear these two phrases chanted or sung as the couple walks back down the aisle. You can shout "Mazel tov!" too, if you feel like it.

Following the breaking of the glass, Larry and Susan walk back up the aisle. Some guests may throw confetti or rice (rice is a symbol of fertility and expresses the hope that the couple will heed the command in Genesis to "be fruitful and multiply").

At this point, the couple may spend a few minutes sequestered, just the two of them. This period is called *yichud*. It is a time of seclusion and bonding and is symbolic of the groom bringing the bride into their home.

The wedding reception or dinner now begins. The Talmud advises that we must add to the new couple's joy at the wedding, and thus it is not uncommon for guests to entertain the bride and groom with toasts, songs, and skits—even juggling. At one wedding I attended, the bride's brother sang a song he had written titled, "I Can't Believe Somebody Actually Married My Sister."

During the celebration, the band plays some spirited and traditional Jewish music; happy (and, hopefully, strong) friends seat the newlyweds in chairs and hoist them up in the air. This is one of those things that occurs at most Jewish weddings, and everyone—sometimes even the bride and groom—loves it. I have yet to see anyone dropped; I hope you won't either.

A Jewish wedding is full of rich cultural and religious traditions. If you know what to look for, the experience is even more rewarding. Hope you had a good time!

Let's Go to a Circumcision!

You've been invited to a very unusual social gathering. A few days ago your friend Ellen gave birth to her first baby—a boy. As her neighbor and friend, you've supported her during the pregnancy, visited her in the hospital, helped out with meals when she first got home, and bought presents for little Seth. Now Ellen tells you there will be a *brit* later this week at her home, and she and her husband Phil would like you to attend the ritual circumcision (it may also be referred to as a *bris* or *brit milah*).

Most of us are familiar with the concept of circumcision, but the concept of performing surgery of this special nature in a family's house may be a little difficult to fathom. However, since you're always open to new experiences, and Ellen assures you that this is typical for Jewish people, you say, "Sure, why not. I'll be there."

Let's go right to the source to find the reason for the circumcision ritual: "This is my covenant, which you shall keep, between me and you and your offspring after you: Every male among you shall be circumcised" (Genesis 17:10). This is followed by: "You shall circumcise the flesh of your foreskins, and it shall be a sign of the covenant between me and you. . . . So shall my covenant be in your flesh an everlasting covenant" (Genesis 17:11,13).

The circumcision ritual was first practiced by Abraham, who, at the age of ninety-nine, circumcised himself and all the men in his household. He circumcised his son Isaac when the boy was eight days old. (The Jewish people perform the circumcision on the eighth day instead of the ninety-ninth year, for obvious reasons.)

Circumcision is one of the oldest rituals in Judaism, and through the centuries it was the one feature that physically distinguished Jews from everyone else. Jews who are not particularly "Jewish" in their lifestyles and behavior have their sons circumcised. Even during times of persecution (including the Holocaust), the practice continued. This ritual is a covenant between the Jewish people and God, and that is the only reason or explanation that is needed to justify it.

The Jewish people did not invent circumcision; it has been practiced widely through the centuries and throughout the world by many tribes, cultures, and religions. Few groups circumcised their sons as early in life, however, as the Jews; in many cultures, circumcision was and is a rite of puberty.

Over the years studies have shown that certain types of cancer occur less frequently in circumcised males and their sexual partners. The vast majority of men in the United States are circumcised, although the medical debate about its benefits and advisability sway one way and the other. Regardless of the associated health benefits and of the hue and cry regularly heard against the act of circumcision, it remains to the Jewish people a religious issue, and a serious one. It is interesting to note that many Soviet Jews who were not circumcised as children because of religious persecution chose to undergo the ritual as adults once they left the Soviet Union.

Besides Phil (the father), Ellen (the mother), and Seth (the son), there are several other principal players. There is the *mohel* (often pronounced "moil," which is the Yiddish pronunciation— this is the person who will perform the procedure), the *sandek* (the person who will hold the child during the ritual), and a couple who perform a role similar to that of godparents in the Christian tradition. If we are going to play this by the book, the godmother takes the child from the mother, hands him off to the godfather, who makes a lateral pass to the father, who then delivers the child to the sandek. This complicated transferal is necessary because of biblical and traditional rules regarding con-tact between the mother and the father in the days immediately following childbirth. The result of all this is that much of the family is included in the ceremony, which occurs, as mentioned above, eight days after the birth of the baby (barring health complications).

Circumcision is considered such an important rite that it is permitted on the Sabbath or on Yom Kippur (the holiest day of the year).

While any competent surgeon can perform the circumcision procedure, the mohel is a specialist in this particular religious and surgical procedure. Although generally not a medical doc-tor, the mohel is trained and highly experienced. Interestingly, in England there is a long-standing tradition that the principal mohel in London performs circumcisions on the male children of the royal family.

Back at Ellen and Phil's house, Seth has been passed carefully from his mother to the sandek via the other players. The role of sandek is usually given to a grandfather or other close relative or friend of the family and is considered a great honor. The sandek's job is to hold the child, who is typically secured on a little carrier to prevent undue movement.

The mohel recites the necessary prayers, including a special blessing that gives the child his Hebrew name—one he will use at the time of his bar mitzvah, his wedding, and all other religious occasions. Just before the circumcision, the mohel explains the procedure, the use of traditional and modern instruments, and that the baby will be uncomfortable only briefly. The surgery is then performed *very* quickly, after which the baby is given to Ellen to be nursed. The ceremony is followed by guests sharing refreshments or a meal.

One interesting ritual that is sometimes observed dates back to biblical times and involves the redemption of the firstborn son. Practiced mostly by Orthodox and some Conservative Jews, it is called *pidyon haben* in Hebrew. According to the story of Exodus, ten plagues were visited on the ancient Egyptians before the Jews were freed from slavery, the tenth being the slaying of the firstborn sons. Because God spared the firstborn sons of the Jews, these boys were seen as *belonging* to God and were given special ritual duties and responsibilities. Later, these duties were turned over to the Kohanim (the priests, descendants of Aaron), and the firstborn sons were relieved of those responsibilities. In a ceremonial rite, a person of Kohanim descent offers the boy's father the choice of a small sum of "silver" *or* the child. The father, for some reason, always chooses the baby, and the Kohen then donates the money to charity. This ceremony takes place on the thirty-first day after birth.

Little Seth has been circumcised. The covenant with God has been kept, and you have shared in a most significant Jewish experience.

Baby Namings and Rituals for Daughters

As I mentioned previously, baby boys are named at the time of their circumcision ceremony. Since there is no parallel ritual for girls, through the years ceremonies have been created to honor and celebrate the birth of a daughter.

It is typical for a girl infant to have a naming ceremony during the Shabbat service immediately following her birth, or at the first service that mother and child are able to attend. Many ceremonies, however, are held in the home several weeks or months after the birth. There are a variety of ceremonies celebrating the birth of a daughter, among them are *brit habat* ("covenant for the daughter") and *simchat habat* ("celebration of the daughter").

At the synagogue, the parents may be honored with an *aliyah* (being called up to recite a prayer before and after the reading of portions of the Torah on Shabbat), and other members of the family may participate as well. When the blessing is recited that gives the baby her Hebrew name, the name is used along with the Hebrew name of the father and (these days) the mother. (Rituals and holy books, such as the aliyah and the Torah, are discussed fully in other chapters.)

The ceremony may also take place in the home (it is not necessary that it take place on the eighth day). You can assume that all major life cycle events include a *seudat mitzvah* ("meal of the mitzvah"). Whether it's simple or fancy, a potluck or a catered affair, there will be food, and this remains a theme through many Jewish ceremonies, holidays, and rituals.

The act of naming and being named is a serious one. In the Bible, when Abram and Sarai accepted the covenant of God, their names were changed to Abraham and Sarah. The name of their grandson, Jacob (the first Jewish baby), became Israel.

Ashkenazic Jews have traditionally named their children after deceased relatives (see "Ashkenazic and Sephardic Jews"). This is considered an honor to the departed person, and because Jews have a Hebrew name as well as the name they use in everyday life, the honor can be done without saddling the child with a name that may be unfashionable or difficult to carry. Often the two names are linked in some way, perhaps by the first letter or syllable. For example, a boy might have the name Sean or Stephen, but his Hebrew name might be Shlomo or Solomon. The Hebrew name is used during religious rituals—at the bar or bat mitzvah, as part of the Jewish wedding ceremony, when being called to the Torah, and at the person's religious funeral service.

Superstition abounds in baby namings. For example, parents might not want to name a child after a relative who died in an accident, had trouble with the law, or was unsuccessful or chronically ill. However, a child may be named after a relative who had special qualities: "She should be as kind, talented, and intelligent as her Grandma Eva was."

At one time Ashkenazic Jews (in contrast to Sephardic Jews) believed that naming a child after a living person might cause the early death of the adult whose name was used. As a result of this belief, very few Jewish people have "Jr." after their names—in my entire life I've known only one. Another belief was that the angel of death, coming to take the older relative, might mistakenly take the child with the same name. As a result, children of Ashkenazic Jewish descent are generally named after deceased relatives only. The reason given is that it "honors" the deceased relative, but the tradition is a result of the taboo.

Another Ashkenazic custom was to change the name of a sick child in order to fool the evil spirit that was causing the illness. A friend of mine told me that her mother once suffered a severe childhood illness, prompting her parents to change her name. She subsequently recovered, grew to adulthood, and eventually gave birth to my friend.

As we all know, when it comes to angels of death and evil spirits, it's better to play it on the safe side.

Adoption

The act of adopting a child is not unknown in the Bible. The rescue and subsequent rearing of Moses by Pharaoh's daughter is an integral part of the story leading up to the Exodus. Like most things Jewish, the concept and process of adoption proceed from traditional Jewish law to a more liberal interpretation of that law.

In Judaism, the process of adopting a child closely parallels the rituals following the birth of a child, but with a few exceptions.

If the birth mother was Jewish, then the child is automatically considered Jewish also. If the birth mother was not Jewish, then, as unusual as it may sound, it is necessary for the child to go through a conversion process.

The conversion process may include, for both boys and girls, a ritual immersion in the mikvah, the special religious bath (see "Shabbat—The Sabbath"). If the child is a newborn boy, a brit milah (circumcision) may be performed on the eighth day after birth, at which time the baby receives his Hebrew name.

However, the brit may take place at a later date, following the legal adoption procedures. A baby girl may receive her Hebrew name following the mikvah ceremony or at a later synagogue ceremony.

If an older child is adopted, and the birth mother was not Jewish, the mikvah ceremony is still a part of the conversion process, but a boy's circumcision will generally be done in a clinical setting with appropriate anesthesia, with both a physician and a mohel participating. Had the boy already received a nonreligious circumcision, then the brit is more symbolic. (A drop of blood may be drawn from the site of the circumcision by the mohel as blessings are recited. This is similar to the ritual performed when an adult male converts to Judaism.)

The Jewish law is interpreted differently by more liberal rabbis and congregations in contemporary Jewish society. For example, the Reform movement recognizes children born to either a Jewish father or a Jewish mother as being Jewish. This, of course, changes the picture a bit. In addition, many rabbis and congregations consider a child who is raised as a Jew in a Jewish home to be Jewish regardless of whether a ritual conversion ceremony has taken place.

Thus, Jewish adoption falls into the category of things that should not be attempted without first consulting a professional—in this case, a rabbi.

An Invitation to a Bar Mitzvah and a Bat Mitzvah

Unless you are Jewish, what would bring you to the synagogue on the Sabbath to attend a Jewish religious service?

As luck would have it, one day the mail brings you an invitation to attend a combination bar mitzvah and bat mitzvah, and you are about to experience a traditional Jewish Sabbath service.

You work with Naomi, and over the years the two of you have become friends. At various times, you've met her husband, Steve, and their two children, David and Lisa, who are just about to turn thirteen. David and Lisa are fraternal twins.

Although not a typical occurrence, this double ceremony, referred to as *b'nai mitzvah,* is not unheard of, and it will allow me to describe more easily the ceremonies for both girls and boys. I have cousins whose son and daughter celebrated their b'nai mitzvah together, and it was a wonderful event.

Let's assume you've never attended a bar mitzvah or bat mitzvah before and that you know very little about the rituals or what is expected of you as a guest.

The invitation announces that in a few weeks, on a Saturday morning at 10:00 A.M. at a nearby synagogue, Lisa and David will be called to the Torah, and you are invited to share the experience. You are also invited to a reception to be held that evening at a local social club.

You won't be the only non-Jewish person at the service—many of Steve and Naomi's non-Jewish friends will be there. We assume that the ceremony will be held at either a Conservative or a Reform synagogue. (In an Orthodox synagogue, the women sit separately from the men and the ceremony is primarily in Hebrew. Girls celebrate a bat mitzvah around the time of their twelfth birthday. Girls have not, in the past, been called to the Torah, but there are signs that this tradition may be changing.)

The ritual takes place on a Saturday, the Jewish Sabbath. While very observant Jews do not drive on the Sabbath, most Jews do. Some of the congregants are dressed very casually, and others dress up more. (Times, fashions, and customs have changed—men used to wear a suit and tie when attending a baseball game. I recommend that when going to the synagogue you dress conservatively and in a manner appropriate for a religious service.)

I suggest that you not bring gifts to the synagogue. It is entirely acceptable to send gifts before or after the event. If you're going to the evening reception, you may bring a gift with you at that time—usually a table is set up for this purpose. Checks or savings bonds are appropriate gifts; people will be going up to David and Lisa with envelopes all night. Besides the religious ceremony, it is very close to their thirteenth birthdays.

Some congregants show up at the synagogue early and are present primarily for the religious service, not the bar and bat mitzvah per se. Depending on the frequency of the family's participation at the synagogue, regular attendees may not know David and Lisa from Adam and Eve. Steve and Naomi are probably members of the congregation, but they may or may not be active members.

Near the entrance to the sanctuary where the services will take place is a box filled with small, black skullcaps called *kippot* (singular, *kippah*; this cap is also known by the Yiddish term *yarmulke*—see "Religious Apparel and Dress"). Return the kippah to the box on your way out. Often, kippot come in colors other than black and are personalized with the name of the bar/bat mitzvah child; it is OK to keep these after you use them.

If the congregation is Reform, it is not required that men wear a head covering, but many do. In Conservative synagogues, all men (including non-Jewish men), generally wear kippot when in the sanctuary, and many women wear kippot, hats or hair coverings. In Orthodox congregations, married women (and all males) cover their heads.

You are now seated comfortably in the sanctuary. A prayer book was given to you when you walked in, or there is one in a compartment in front of your seat or on your chair. Note that the book says something like "Sabbath and Holiday Prayer Book." On the right-hand page is Hebrew, which looks like Greek to you. On the left-hand page is English. Unless you're in Buenos Aires, in which case the left-hand page is in Spanish.

Family members—including parents, siblings, grandparents, and other close relatives—are (or soon will be) seated in the front rows. Everyone seems happy, as well they should. This is a very joyous occasion for the family, and many out-of-town relatives and guests have traveled long distances to share the event. Lisa and David are soon to participate in a ceremony that proclaims that they have become adults in the eyes of the congregation and the Jewish world. Now, we are aware that they are only thirteen and may know little about life other than what they learn in the eighth grade and on cable television. They can't drive, vote, or even buy a lottery ticket, but this is as good a place as any to begin adulthood.

During the religious service, which may last two or three hours, these two young people will lead or assist the congregation in an assortment of prayers and blessings. They will also read a portion of the Torah. The Torah, the holiest of all objects, is a handwritten scroll containing the Five Books of Moses (the Pentateuch). Lisa and David have likely spent a fair number of years learning about Jewish culture, heritage, and lifestyle, as well as how to read and recite Hebrew.

What is this ceremony all about?

The term *bar mitzvah* is Hebrew for "son of the commandment," and *bat mitzvah* means "daughter of the commandment." The term *b'nai mitzvah* means "children of the commandment."

The Mishnah (a compendium of early Jewish law; see "The Torah and the Law") tells us, "At the age of thirteen, one is obliged to observe the commandments." It means that one may now be counted as part of the minyan (quorum) for purposes of group prayer and must also take responsibility as an adult to keep the Sabbath, fast on special holidays, pray, and keep the commandments as an adult. In fact, the word *bar* also means "subject to," so it can be said that *bar mitzvah* and *bat mitzvah* mean that the child is now "subject to the commandments."

Thirteen was probably chosen because it coincides with the average onset of male puberty. Whether you have an elaborate ritual celebration, a simple one, or none at all, at age thirteen a Jewish person "becomes subject to the commandments."

The earliest bar mitzvah ceremonies were quite simple—a boy would read a Torah portion and a *haftarah* portion (a section from the Prophets), and then, perhaps, offer a discourse on some aspect of the Talmud (a collection of scholarly commentary and analysis). His father would then thank God for releasing him of the obligation of taking care of his son.

The concept of the bat mitzvah, the ceremony for girls, did not occur until the twentieth century. Credit for initiating the ritual is given to Mordecai Kaplan, the founder of the Reconstructionist movement, whose daughter Judith celebrated the first recorded bat mitzvah in 1922.

Bat mitzvah ceremonies are sometimes celebrated at age twelve, which is considered the average onset of female puberty. Over the years, the differences between the bar and bat mitzvah have diminished, and in most non-Orthodox congregations today they are identical.

It is not uncommon these days to hear of adults celebrating a bar or bat mitzvah. Many of these adults, women in particular, were not able to celebrate the ritual as children and now feel the desire to experience this rite of "coming of age." In addition, adults converting to Judaism may also choose to celebrate a bar or bat mitzvah.

Many teenagers and adults travel to Israel, where the bar or bat mitzvah ritual might take place at the Western Wall in Jerusalem or at the ruins of Masada. Others celebrate the service in their home. Regardless of the location, the experience is generally a very meaningful one.

We are back at our b'nai mitzvah. David and Lisa have been invited to take seats on the bimah (the raised platform in the front of the sanctuary) next to the rabbi (who may wear a black robe during services). Often the cantor leads the congregation in many prayers and does much of the singing.

The service you are attending today is a typical Saturday morning Shabbat (Sabbath) service, with special time included for the b'nai mitzvah. (The congregation holds a religious service regardless of whether a bar or bat mitzvah is scheduled.)

Lisa and David's grandparents present each child with a tallit, the traditional prayer shawl that must be worn when reciting from the Torah. Regardless of the color, size, or style of the tallit, it has four corners, and at each corner is a fringe (called *tzitzit*). Why fringes? "The LORD said to Moses: Speak to the Israelites, and tell them to make fringes on the corners of their garments . . . So you shall remember and do all my commandments, and you shall be holy to your God" (Numbers 15:37–38, 40).

The twins recite the special prayer for the tallit, kiss the corners of their garments, and put them on.

David and Lisa lead certain prayers in Hebrew and English, and there is responsive reading (the leader reads a phrase, the congregation responds with the next one, and so on). All the prayers speak of the greatness of God and how fortunate we are to have God. If you feel comfortable doing so, you may want to participate in the responsive readings in English. You may find the passages spiritually uplifting and inspirational.

At the center of the bimah is a large cabinet called the ark. Above the ark hangs a light called the *ner tamid* (eternal light), a reminder of the light that burned in Solomon's temple in Jerusalem (see "The Temple"). It is always kept lit.

The ark is representative of the tabernacle that held the stone tablets brought down by Moses from Mount Sinai and carried by the Israelites after their Exodus from Egypt. The ark contains the Torah. (Very often, there is more than one Torah scroll, each presented to the synagogue as a special gift by an individual, family, or group.)

Periodically throughout the service, the doors to the ark are opened, and the congregation is asked to rise. Whenever the ark is opened or the Torah is "standing," the congregation must stand also. At one point, the ark is opened and a Torah is removed. The congregation exuberantly sings a prayer as the Torah is carried around the room—Jews are happy to have been chosen to receive the Torah (this is where the phrase "Chosen People" originated; see the section "The Chosen People"). As the Torah is carried around the room in a procession, adults and children reach out with their prayer books or the corners of their tallit to touch the covered scroll and then kiss the prayer book or tallit.

The Torah is returned to the front of the room, the coverings are removed (there is generally a decorated silver breastplate, two little crowns on the scroll turners, and a pointer), and it is set on a reading lectern. Since the Torah is now "sitting," the congregation can sit, too. (This up-and-down, sitting and standing business is common to all Jewish religious services.)

Next, the Torah portion for the day is read. Reading from the Torah occurs four times every week—on Monday, on Thursday, and at two separate services on Shabbat. Depending on the size of the portion read, a cycle of Torah reading is completed in one to three years. At the end of the cycle, we start again at the beginning. A bar or bat mitzvah may take place on any of the days that the Torah is read.

In some congregations, grandparents and parents are invited up to the bimah, where the Torah scroll is passed "from one generation to the next," symbolizing the importance of passing the religious tradition down to one's children.

As the Torah reading begins, we switch to another book (look for a copy near your chair) that is larger and contains the first five books of the Bible (the Torah), the haftarah sections, and commentary, also in Hebrew and English. During the service, page numbers are announced periodically so you can follow along in Hebrew (you mean you can't read Hebrew?) or you can read the adjacent English text. If you have attended a Christian Sunday school you will soon see that it's the same Old Testament you're familiar with. Although the translation is different (it's not the King James version), the stories are the same— Adam and Eve, Jonah and the whale, Sodom and Gomorrah, and so on.

The Torah is divided into fifty-four sections. Each of these sections is divided into even smaller portions. Of the portions to be read today, Lisa and David will read the last, known as the *maftir*, which means "the one who concludes."

Selected family members and close friends have been given the honor (known in Hebrew as *aliyah)* of reciting a special ritual blessing before and after each Torah portion is read. (Remember that these procedures vary from congregation to congregation.)

In many (but not all) congregations, the first aliyah is reserved for a Kohen—someone directly descended from Aaron, the brother of Moses (Aaron and his descendants were the priests in early Jewish history; refer to the sections "The Temple" and "Jewish Priests").

In the same manner, the second aliyah is reserved for a Levi, a descendent of people who attended the priests. The remaining *aliyot* (plural of aliyah) may be given to people who fall into either of the aforementioned categories or who are members of the third category, Israelite, whose members are descended from the tribes of either Benjamin or Judah. In total, there are seven aliyot portions on Shabbat. Some congregations add an extra aliyah for the person who reads the haftarah, very often the person celebrating the bar or bat mitzvah.

It is also considered an honor to open and close the doors to the ark and to hold or tend to the Torah at the necessary times. The names of all who receive these honors are announced to the congregation, and on completion of the reading or task, the so-honored person receives congratulations and handshakes from other congregants.

Now it is David and Lisa's turn. Once again the special prayer before the Torah reading is recited, and then first one and then the other reads a portion of the appropriate Torah section. The Hebrew as written in the Torah contains no vowels and must be sung or chanted in a specific manner, which makes it all the more difficult. Occasionally the reader can stop for a moment to discuss the correct pronunciation of a word with others nearby. Since the twins have practiced their particular sections for months, interruptions are unlikely.

After the reading of the Torah comes the reading of the haftarah. This is a special portion from one of the books of the Prophets. Many people believe that the reading of this portion originated at a time in history when Jews were forbidden to read the actual Torah under the penalty of death (penalties and death are recurring themes in Jewish history). Thus, a passage was chosen from other works that in some way reflected the Torah reading. The haftarah is often about familiar Biblical characters.

It is interesting that references to this portion of the service appear in the New Testament—Luke 4:17 tells us that Jesus was given the scroll of the prophet Isaiah to read as part of the Sabbath service at the synagogue in Nazareth.

After the completion of Lisa's and David's haftarah portions, we all breathe a big sigh of relief! Their major obligations for the day are complete, and everyone is very happy.

The Torah scroll is raised (we stand), rolled, bound, dressed, and then carried around the room as congregants sing and clap their hands. The Torah is then returned to the ark (we sit).

The rabbi discusses the content of the day's readings, speaks directly to David and Lisa about the importance and responsibility of being Jewish adults, and recites a special blessing for them.

Naomi and Steve then recount the many trials and tribulations of the *b'nai mitzvah* experience and speak about what great kids they have, what fun it has been raising twins, what sacrifices each family member has made, who was of special help during the process, and how everyone's lives changed during the last year. Individually, Lisa and David (suddenly "adults") reflect on the meaningfulness of the day and what was learned from the experience. They thank the rabbi, the cantor, the Hebrew teacher, their parents, their siblings, and other relatives.

I can tell you from personal experience that having a child become a bar mitzvah or bat mitzvah is a major life experience, and everyone comes away from it having changed and, hopefully, grown.

A word of caution—usually there is no applause in the synagogue! Laughter is OK, as are tears, both of which you will hear and see; trust me. Friends and family often throw candy or flowers at the conclusion of the ceremony. A final song and prayer conclude the service, and the family (first) and then the congregants leave the sanctuary and reassemble in another room to recite blessings over wine and challah (bread). Refreshments, such as fruit, cookies, etc., are offered, depending on the custom of the congregation or what the family has decided to prepare. In some cases lunch may be served.

A few words on bar and bat mitzvah celebrations: typically, the family hosts a party or reception, which can be small and intimate or large and beyond one's imagination. While there may be some religious aspects to the party (a prayer over the wine and bread, lighting of candles, and some traditional Jewish music and dancing), remember that the actual bar or bat mitzvah ritual has been completed. It is a celebration and a wonderful opportunity for out-of-town relatives and friends to reunite and share the joyous occasion.

Whether the party is simple, lavish, or extravagant, enjoy yourself!

A Jewish Funeral—Saying Good-bye to Uncle Harry

Even you called him Uncle Harry.

The sweet, elderly gentleman lived in one of the ground-floor units of your apartment complex, and you spent many pleasant moments chatting with him on his small patio. He told stories about his childhood in Eastern Europe, his emigration and life in the United States as a young man, his marriage, his successful career in the retail clothing business, his activities within the local Jewish community, his travels, his children and grandchildren, and his numerous girlfriends since the death of his wife fifteen years earlier.

In the last year or so he'd grown less active; surgery and a mild stroke had slowed him down even more. You and other neighbors would pick things up for him at the grocery store and prepare a few simple meals when necessary. His daughter appreciated all this since she lived forty-five minutes away. Uncle Harry had gone into the hospital a few days before, and you were not very surprised to get a phone call from his daughter letting you know of his death and inviting you to attend the service and funeral to be held the next day.

The first stage of mourning for relatives of the deceased is to make all arrangements necessary for the burial. This stage is of major concern, precludes other activities and commandments of Judaism, and lasts from the death to the burial.

Under Jewish custom, the body will not be left alone from the time of death until the burial.

(Autopsies have traditionally not been permitted under Jewish law because they are viewed as a desecration of the body. However, donation of organs or the entire body for medical purposes is more common today than before, falling under the Jewish principle that saving a life is more important than the keeping of many other laws.)

You arrive at the Jewish funeral home. Some of Uncle Harry's relatives thank you for coming and help you find a seat in the chapel. In the past, close relatives would rend (tear) a garment they were wearing as a sign of mourning and symbolic of the tearing that had occurred in their lives following the loss of a loved one. On this day, each mourner wears a black ribbon, symbolically torn, pinned to the clothing.

By the way, flowers are not sent for Jewish funerals and you will probably not see them at the Jewish funeral parlor. It is believed that because non-Jews historically were not necessarily buried soon after death and/or were embalmed, flowers were used at these funerals to offset any odors emanating from the body. Jews, however, were (and are) not embalmed—the Bible suggests that the body should be buried in the earth from which it came in its original state, and Jewish law requires burial within twenty-four hours of death ("you shall bury him that same day" [Deuteronomy 21:23]). Thus, the use of flowers never became a Jewish custom. A Jewish funeral can be delayed until close relatives arrive, but the burial is almost always within three days of death.

At the service, a longtime friend of Uncle Harry's delivers a heartfelt eulogy expressing Harry's goodness, his contributions to society, Harry's love for his family, and the loss that is felt by friends and loved ones. The blessing recited is, "Blessed are You, O Lord our God, Ruler of the universe, the True Judge."

The coffin is a simple wooden one. This is in keeping with the Jewish concept of avoiding situations in which relatives feel compelled to outdo the expensive funerals of well-to-do neighbors. The coffin is closed. It is not considered respectful to view the body of the deceased.

Through the ages, cremation was not acceptable according to Jewish law and therefore never became part of the Jewish tradition. As a result of the tragedies of the Holocaust, many Jews consider the practice of cremation to be distasteful. Despite this tradition, however, some liberal Jews today are cremated after death. Orthodox and Conservative Jewish cemeteries do not allow for the burial of cremation ashes.

After friends and relatives have shared some incredibly funny and tender reminiscences about Uncle Harry, a hearse takes his body to the cemetery, and you and many others follow in cars.

At the graveside, you all regroup. There are chairs situated under a canopy that is open at the sides. The rabbi reads selected psalms and the mourners recite the Kaddish—the mourner's prayer that indicates faith, distress, and submission to the will of God. (Observant Jews recite the Kaddish prayer daily for up to a year after the death of a family member.)

After the casket is placed in the ground, many people (including you) pass by and toss a small amount of earth into the opening or simply pat the earth down a bit. This is a way of saying a final good-bye—it is considered an honor as well as an obligation to help bury the dead. You may recite a prayer that asks for God's forgiveness of anyone who may have wronged the deceased. Then the mourners leave the cemetery, often walking between two rows of the remaining attendees who offer words of condolence.

Uncle Harry's daughter asks you to join family and friends at her home after the service. It is customary to wash your hands before entering the home after a visit to the cemetery. This is a symbolic washing, and there may be a little bowl of water near the entrance to the house for this purpose. Food is served, and often bread and hard-boiled eggs are included in the "meal of condolence"; the round egg symbolizes the ongoing cycle of human life. (The afterlife is discussed in "Creation, Heaven, Hell, and Life after Death".)

Uncle Harry's family now enters the next stage of mourning called *shivah* (this means "seven"). The family is said to be "sitting shivah" during the seven-day period that begins on the day of the funeral. It is during this period that friends and relatives will "pay a shivah (condolence) call."

Officially, mourners include only the deceased's parents, children, siblings, and spouse. Adherence to religious customs and traditions varies from family to family, depending on their cultural background and level of religious observance.

During the first week of mourning, very observant Jews will not sit on chairs of normal height and may remove sofa cushions in order to sit closer to the floor, a gesture suggesting the depth to which their grief has brought them. Only mourners are required to sit on these low chairs. In addition, observant mourners may not bathe or shower, cut their hair or shave, change their outer garments, wear leather footwear, go to work, or have sexual relations—in other words, all things "pleasurable" (even work!) are to be avoided. Mirrors in the home are covered to prevent "vanity" during the mourning period, although some believe this custom is based on the superstitious belief that the spirit of the deceased, still present in the house, may become confused by its own image and refuse to leave the premises.

At the home of more observant mourners, religious services may be performed three times a day and require a minyan. (The minyan prayer quorum is described in "Prayers and Blessings.") This is necessary because some mourners choose to not leave the house during the seven days of shivah, but would still like to participate in a service.

It is important to note that while many or all of these traditional requirements of mourning may be followed, everything depends on a person's level of religious belief. Reform Jews, for example, may not be as strict in their observance of the mourning rituals and often limit the period of shivah to three days. The practice of observing a shorter shivah period is increasingly common among Conservative Jews as well.

In some homes, a large candle burns during the entire shivah period. Family members and neighbors visit the mourners, bringing meals and keeping the family company. "Paying a shivah call" is considered a *mitzvah* (a "commandment") as much as a "good deed." Visitors may enter the home without knocking, and it is not necessary to go out of your way to express your condolences—it is enough just to be there, to reflect the mood, and to help console the mourners.

The thirty days following the burial (including the seven-day shivah period) is called *sheloshim,* and while many of the "bans" against participating in "pleasurable" activities are lifted (it's OK now to have sex), many Jews continue to abstain from certain social functions, such as going to parties and other events. Some attend religious services to recite the Kaddish prayer on a daily basis. However, on the thirtieth day, all of the mourning-related restrictions end. The one exception is for people who have lost a parent. For them, the mourning period, called *avelut* (literally "mourning"), continues for a Jewish calendar year, starting from the day of the death. More observant Jews recite the Kaddish prayer at daily and/or weekly religious services for eleven of these months. (The Jewish calendar is described in the section "Holidays and the Jewish Calendar".)

It is important to note that regardless of how long the mourning period is, public mourning is not observed on the Sabbath. Since Shabbat is a day for expressing joy, it is important that even death not intrude on this day. So, even though we are still grieving, the mourning process is "suspended" until the conclusion of Shabbat.

The anniversary of the death of the relative (*Yahrzeit*) is recalled each year with the lighting of a Yahrzeit candle and a prayer. This reminds us that Judaism stresses that life is sacred and that we should not forget those who once played a vital role in our lives. This candle is also lighted on the eve of Yom Kippur. Some people also light a Yahrzeit candle at the end of other festivals such as Passover, Shavuot, and Sukkot.

As with all other Jewish practices and rituals, how a Jewish person mourns the death of a loved one varies greatly from person to person and from family to family.

Within a year after the death, members of the immediate family may gather at the cemetery to participate in an "unveiling" of the recently placed gravestone or marker, which is generally of simple design. Visitors to the grave often leave a pebble at the site indicating that someone has been there to remember the departed. (When I visited the tomb of David Ben-Gurion, the first prime minister of Israel and one of the founders of the modern Israeli state, many pebbles rested on his gravestone.)

As you leave her home, Uncle Harry's daughter thanks you for attending the service and for being good to him while he was alive. You will miss him, as will we all.

You Can Only Get a Divorce If You're Married

It is written in the Jewish literature, "Even the altar [God] sheds tears when anyone divorces his wife" (the Talmud, Sanhedrin 22a). Thus, divorce is not encouraged in Judaism. The Talmud is also very clear, though, that a divorce is called for when a marriage is unhealthy. In the past, divorce among Jews was rare, but these days the Jewish divorce rate is similar to that of the general population.

So while divorce is not encouraged, it is permitted in Judaism, and obtaining a Jewish divorce (as opposed to a civil divorce) is as filled with tradition and ceremony, albeit solemn, as are any of the other milestones in life. Remember, except under special circumstances, a Jewish divorce is recognized only by Jewish law—a couple may obtain a civil divorce and still be considered married under Jewish law, and the reverse is also true.

A bill of Jewish divorce is called a *get*. If a divorced Jew wishes to remarry within the Jewish religion and wants to follow the letter of the Jewish law, then he or she must obtain a get. Only about 10 percent of Jewish couples that pursue a divorce go through the process of a formal Jewish divorce.

The husband is generally the party who must "officially" initiate the dissolution of the marriage, and he must have the consent of his wife. Agreement by both parties is necessary, but a Jewish religious court can compel a husband to grant a divorce under certain circumstances (abuse, lack of support, adultery, and so on). The court can also decide that the wife's refusal to accept the get is unjustified and can permit the man to remarry. These sorts of things usually come up after the couple has obtained a civil divorce and one of the parties has remarried without the couple having obtained a Jewish divorce.

Jewish tradition tells us that it is better for children to live with a divorced parent than to grow up in a home filled with enmity and discord. Issues regarding custody of children, division of property, and spousal support are generally worked out as part of the civil divorce.

I have personal experience with the process of Jewish divorce, having obtained a get approximately ten years after my civil divorce. Although I am not an Orthodox Jew, I visited the home of an Orthodox rabbi and spent more than four hours observing and being a party to the get procedure.

After a lengthy and detailed history of my Jewish upbringing, education, religious marriage ceremony, and civil divorce, the rabbi brought me from his study to another room (it was actually his dining room) that contained a large table. Around the table sat several young men working with special pens and ink on parchmentlike paper.

The terms of my Jewish divorce were documented by one of the men, performing the role of scribe, as he meticulously wrote out the terms of the dissolution in the get. Checking the document for errors and making sure it was absolutely perfect took what seemed like hours. As a matter of fact, errors are often intentionally introduced during the process so that they can be corrected later—no one but God produces anything that's perfect.

Following this was a lengthy and very formal procedure in which I entrusted one of the young men (a total stranger) with the task of delivering the document to my ex-wife. As required, I specifically gave him instructions to use whatever means necessary, including the use of up to one hundred agents, to complete the task! At one point during this solemn and very serious process, I had to stifle a smile as I envisioned a hundred young, bearded, Orthodox secret agents scurrying about behind bushes and parked cars with the sole mission of delivering the document to my ex.

In reality, the get was shipped to a rabbi in another city, and he made arrangements to personally deliver the document. Thus was the finale to my religious divorce procedures. In an odd way, it provided me with a sense of closure to the relationship, something that had not occurred after my civil divorce.

In theory, the wife is paid whatever was promised in the *ketubbah* (the Jewish marriage decree); this may be a symbolic amount. Once again, however, the civil court is the real arbiter of child and spousal support and custody issues.

The Reform movement recognizes a civil divorce as sufficient and does not necessarily require a get for remarriage within it's own movement. Because of this, I found it interesting that the

Reform rabbi who performed my second marriage was quite concerned that my new wife's get proceeded according to tradition. (I believe this had to do with the language in her original ketubbah.)

The situation can become even more complex if a divorced Reform Jew wishes to marry a person who is a Conservative or Orthodox Jew. In this case, a get is generally required because the religious legitimacy of children born into the new marriage would be affected. This is a very complicated issue, best left to Jewish legal scholars. But when has divorce not been a complicated issue?

Home Life, Jewish Beliefs, and Other Interesting Matters

Is a Kosher Hot Dog
Really Kosher?

What is kosher? What does the word *kosher* mean? If you see a hot dog stand on the corner, and a sign reads, "Kosher Hot Dogs," are the hot dogs really kosher? If you buy a package of Hebrew National kosher hot dogs at the supermarket, are they kosher?

If a Jewish person who keeps a kosher home buys the package of kosher hot dogs, takes them home, prepares a few, and serves them to you, they are kosher from the moment the animal they were made from was ritually slaughtered to the moment that the hot dogs are eaten. If someone else buys the package of hot dogs and brings it home, they will be kosher until they're opened and then hit the cooking pan. Why?

The whole concept of *kashrut* (dietary laws) hinges not on health factors, as many people think, but on belief itself. Certain statements in the Torah must be obeyed even though it is not clearly explained why they must be obeyed. This category of mandatory statutes is known as *hukim* and defies explanation. The observance of the rules of kashrut fall into this category. These beliefs have unified the Jewish people through the centuries and have separated them from their non-Jewish neighbors and the general population. (Forcing observant Jews to eat pork has been a standard form of anti-Semitic torture for centuries.) The rules of kashrut continuously remind Jews of their roots. It is a *mitz-vah* (a commandment and a "good deed") to follow the rules.

Certain dietary restrictions are set down very explicitly in the Bible. Through the years, the Rabbis elaborated on the rules regarding the ritual slaughter of animals, the separation of dairy and meat (through the use of separate sets of dishes, for instance), preparation of the food, and so on. Adherence to these rules is referred to as "keeping kosher." It provides the answer to the question of why the kosher hot dog may no longer be considered kosher once it hits the cooking pan: if the pan has been used for cooking either dairy foods or nonkosher meat, the meal is not kosher.

As a child who was curious about what was kosher, what was not kosher, what could be eaten in combination with what, and why, I received many of the answers that continue to cloud the entire subject. These answers inevitably include factors of cleanliness of the facility where the animals were slaughtered, butchered, prepared, and packaged. Other reasons describe the "bad habits" of the animals themselves: "Pigs eat garbage"; "Lobsters and crabs are scavengers"; or "Insects eat excrement." In the end, I was told whatever the speaker believed to be true or whatever he or she thought would satisfy my curiosity.

If I had been told, "We do it because it's commanded in the Bible—now sit down and don't eat ham," would *that* have satisfied my curiosity? I don't know. The truth is, a kosher diet isn't necessarily a healthier diet. Chicken fat (known as *schmaltz* in Yiddish and used to fry things such as chicken livers and onions) is surely as much an artery clogger as bacon grease (which cannot be rendered kosher) or butter (which can).

The book of Leviticus lists kosher and nonkosher animals, and other sections of the religious writings indicate what is fit for use and how it should be prepared. Exodus 22:31 says, "you shall not eat any meat that is mangled by beasts in the field; you shall throw it to the dogs." This has been interpreted to mean that if an animal was killed in other than a prescribed ritual-slaughtering method, you can't eat it (good-bye to venison shot by your good friend who loves to go hunting).

One of the purposes of the ritual slaughter was certainly to minimize the pain and suffering of the animal. There is more than one biblical reference about preventing cruelty to animals, including the warnings "You shall not muzzle an ox while it is treading out the grain" (Deuteronomy 25:4) and "The righteous know the needs of their animals" (Proverbs 12:10). If it were not for all the specific references to the ritual slaughter of animals, one might think that God meant us all to be vegetarians (some people do, in fact, believe this to be true).

Deuteronomy 14:9–10 informs us, "Of all that live in water you may eat these: whatever has fins and scales you may eat" and "whatever does not have fins and scales you shall not eat" (thus no lobster, butter sauce, and bib). Deuteronomy 14:21 and Exodus 23:19 tell us, "You shall not boil a kid in its mother's milk." The Rabbis interpret this to mean that any mixing of milk and meat is forbidden (adios, cheeseburgers).

Deuteronomy 12:23 commands, "Only be sure that you do not eat the blood; for blood is the life, and you shall not eat the life with the meat." So we are advised to remove as much blood as possible from all meat and poultry before cooking. This involves a process of either soaking the meat in water and salting it or roasting the meat, both of which remove as much blood from the meat as possible. Oddly enough, once the "koshering" process" has been applied to meat, it is considered fit to eat, even raw, like steak tartare!

I want to mention one other food category that is considered "neutral" *(pareve)*. This group includes all fish that have fins and scales and all foods that grow in the earth. The laws of kashrut permit us to eat pareve foods along with either meat or dairy products. A person can be a vegetarian and still be kosher—dairy products can be eaten (by nonvegans) with any fruits and vegetables. If an observant Jewish person eats fish, ovo-lacto products, and vegetables only, he or she can still be strictly kosher *and* have only one set of dishes. Everything that grows from the earth is kosher and pareve, including all grains, fungi, weeds, trees, bushes, flowers, seeds, and nuts.

Fish and aquatic animals not considered kosher include all shellfish, eels, sharks, amphibians, whales, and other sea mammals (adieu to turtle soup, frogs' legs, scampi, and calamari).

If an animal both chews its cud and has a split hoof, it is considered kosher: "Any animal that has divided hoofs and is cleft-footed and chews the cud—such you may eat" (Leviticus 11:3). It's important to know, however, that the animal must also be ritually slaughtered by a specially trained person (called a *shochet*). There is an exception: "The pig, for even though it has divided hoofs and is cleft-footed, it does not chew the cud; it is unclean for you. Of their flesh you shall not eat, and their carcasses you shall not touch; they are unclean for you" (Leviticus 11:7–8).

When we speak of the kosher meat industry, we enter a somewhat complicated arena, one that combines the religious study of the laws and ethics of ritual slaughter with the practical aspects of the butcher's trade. Much emphasis is placed on the inspection of the lungs and other organs of the animal as well as on the knife used (the edge of the blade must be completely free of even the smallest nick that might botch a cutting job). Some Orthodox groups demand even higher and more rigorous levels of practice, and as a result even the kosher slaughterhouse industry is affected by politics.

While many animals fit into the "can be kosher" category (antelope, deer, gazelle, moose, and yak, for example), they must be ritually slaughtered, which means that you must somehow raise it domestically and/or make some provision to get your animal to the shochet. You can see how this might present a problem, as in the case of a moose.

Animals that do not fall into the proper category and cannot be considered kosher at all include pigs, donkeys, horses, camels, rabbits, and rodents. In addition, certain cuts of beef are not considered kosher (this gets very complicated, doesn't it?).

As far as fowl is concerned, most domestic birds can be considered kosher (chickens, ducks, geese—even domesticated songbirds). In general, though, wild birds, including ostrich, owls, eagles, and swans, as well as their eggs, are not kosher.

All nonkosher foods are referred to as being *treif,* Hebrew for "torn to pieces."

A special symbol (called a *heksher*) on a product's label indicates that it is kosher and has been prepared under rabbinic supervision. Nonmeat products, such as wine and other beverages, are also prepared under rabbinic supervision, assuring that the rules of kashrut are not compromised. (Additional symbols indicate that a product is kosher for Passover; see "Passover".)

Please note: "Rabbinic supervision" does not mean that a rabbi is standing by the conveyer belt offering a blessing over every jar of pickles and every package of hot dogs coming down the line. That's not what the process is all about. Kosher food is prepared according to strict rules and under supervision, but it is not blessed food.

For the uninitiated, the rules of kashrut can result in a nightmare of maintaining the appropriate pots and pans, dishes, and cutlery. In a kosher home, there are several sets of each, and you must not use a dish for eating meat if you use it for eating dairy. In addition, during the Passover holiday, kosher households substitute special holiday dinnerware and utensils.

Does every Jew keep a kosher home, have multiple sets of dishes, prepare meat by soaking and salting, never eat food that is treif, turn away from cheeseburgers, scampi, rabbit stew, lobster Cantonese, and escargot? Hardly. Liberal Jews may not adhere to the traditional dietary laws, although many may follow some of the customs because of personal preference or tradition. I know that I do. More conservative Jews will observe the rules to varying degrees.

Even Orthodox Jews who follow the rules of kashrut very strictly may show certain idiosyncrasies as to what and where they will eat. Ultra-Orthodox Hasidic Jews practice kashrut to the nth degree *(glatt* kosher).

Should a Gentile worry about what to serve Jewish dinner guests? My advice is to treat the situation as you would if you suspected that a dinner guest is vegetarian or has any other dietary or health concerns—just ask the guests if they're on any special diet and you'll get an answer. In the end, it goes far beyond the question, "Is a kosher hot dog really kosher?"

Jewish Food

Bagels, lox, gefilte fish, matzo—are these Jewish foods? And does gefilte fish mean "filtered fish?" (When I think of the homemade gefilte fish my grandmother used to prepare, complete with the remnants of bones and skin, I remember wishing that it *had* been filtered.)

Ethnic foods often arise from poverty, limited availability due to climate or distribution, or long-forgotten traditions. This is certainly the case when we refer to the "soul food" created by African slaves in America who had very little to work with, the potatoes and cabbage of the impoverished Irish, or the stuffing of a fish with bread or flour by Jews to make it serve a lot of hungry people *(gefilte,* by the way, means "stuffed").

Each ethnic group brings to the dinner table traditions that may have begun in culinary poverty but have evolved into culinary delights. However, as these traditions continue to evolve, sometimes the product becomes something that would be barely recognizable to the diner who was present during the early days of the dish. For example, how many different shapes and varieties of pasta can you buy these days in the store? Do the "chitlins" of today bear any resemblance to those of 150 years ago? How would the followers of Moses in the desert respond to the commercially prepared matzo you buy in the supermarket at Passover time, each perfectly square and packaged in a cardboard box wrapped in paper and cellophane?

Let me rant about bagels for a moment. Bagels used to be Jewish food. When I was a boy, they were hard, hard, hard. And plain. In them, there were no seeds, nuts, whole grains, cranberries, chocolate chips, and so on. Bagels now come in a million varieties—sometimes even "original." As for lox, the bagel with cream cheese and smoked salmon you order in Honolulu or Cabo San Lucas is definitely not the bagel with cream cheese and lox that I ate as a boy!

Besides the foods that are specific to certain holidays I've mentioned, there are a couple of other foods that evolved in Jewish households. One is kugel, a baked pudding made of either noodles or potatoes, which has always been one of my favorites. My mother would make potato kugel any time I was willing to peel and hand-grate the potatoes. These days my wife, using a food processor, makes an equally wonderful kugel. I still peel the potatoes, though.

Of course, there is challah, the twisted loaf of egg bread, which is served both on Shabbat and during holidays. Bread is closely identified with the general concept of food in many places and cultures, and in Judaism this is also the case; the blessing for food traditionally is said over the challah.

While wandering in the desert and surviving on manna (from heaven), the Israelites were told to gather a double portion the day before the Sabbath, so that they would not be required to work on the day of rest. This double portion is symbolized today by having two loaves of challah (or one regular-sized loaf and a smaller "baby" loaf) on the Shabbat table. Many people refuse to cut the challah with a knife, preferring instead to tear portions off by hand and share smaller pieces of this large portion with many other people. This avoidance of the knife seems to be an extension of the custom of not keeping sharp knives—symbols of war and weapons—on the dinner table. However, I've seen quite a few rabbis use a knife on the challah, so this is obviously not a hard-and-fast rule.

Through the years, in order to encourage the concept of rest and avoid cooking on Shabbat, advance meal preparation became an art and a science. In Eastern European communities, a special type of stew, called *cholent*, was kept warm on the stove over a very low flame throughout the Sabbath. You can still find this dish in the homes of observant Jews on Shabbat. It generally contains beef, barley, beans, and potatoes. In Mediterranean communities, the stew known as *dafina* was served; it consists of chickpeas, potatoes, and other ingredients. In Persia, Jews ate *tbeet*, a combination of rice and chicken.

Any Jewish cookbook offers traditional dishes, but we must always remember that Jews have lived all over the world, and a traditional Jewish dish from Poland probably has little or no resemblance to a traditional Jewish dish from Spain.

One more thing: watch out for bones when you eat your gefilte fish.

Degrees of Orthodoxy

Imentioned earlier a wonderful Shabbat I spent with my friend, an Orthodox Jew, and his family. At about that same time, I was acquainted with another young man who was Orthodox.

Raised in an observant household, he wore a kippah (see "Religious Apparel and Dress") and did not work on Saturday. One Sunday, I saw him walking in a local park with a young woman. The next time I saw him, I asked about her.

He indicated that he would like to get married, and that she was one of a number of women he had dated in the last few years. He said that it was very difficult to find an appropriately Orthodox woman. I was puzzled. He explained that he needed to find someone who was Orthodox—not too Orthodox, but someone of about the same orthodoxy as he. I was more puzzled.

He gave me an example. Some of his Orthodox friends would not eat in a restaurant or at a nonkosher home, but he himself would eat at a non–Orthodox Jewish home if the host would prepare him something like a tuna sandwich on a paper plate using plastic utensils. Many Orthodox women he knew would not wear pants—only skirts or dresses. Deuteronomy tells us, "A woman shall not wear a man's apparel, nor shall a man put on a woman's garment" (Deuteronomy 22:5). He himself felt it was acceptable if a woman wore pants on appropriate occasions. There were other examples; I can't remember what they are, but you get the picture. You're not simply Orthodox or non-Orthodox. There are degrees of variation. I began to understand.

He eventually married and had children. Occasionally his wife wears pants.

Do not confuse Orthodox Judaism with either ultra-Orthodox Judaism or Hasidism. An Orthodox Jew may choose to go to a modern play or other type of entertainment. Hasidic Jews would not attend a show or a play featuring women on stage. More on this later.

Conversion to Judaism

Traditionally, anyone born to a Jewish mother is considered Jewish. Anyone who undergoes formal conversion is also considered Jewish.

For many centuries and in many countries, it has not been easy to be Jewish, and the potential convert must be made aware of the numerous obligations incumbent on a person who contemplates conversion. For this reason, rabbis have often discouraged people from converting to Judaism. However, if a person is persistent, he or she must take certain ritual and educational steps toward conversion.

The majority of people who convert to Judaism in the United States are converted by a rabbi of the Reform or Conservative movements. The potential convert must voluntarily accept the Jewish faith, then follow a course of instruction and study and learn to observe Jewish customs, traditions, and rituals. When the rabbi believes that the person is ready for conversion, a ceremony takes place, the convert receives a Hebrew name, and the person is now considered a Jew. Forever.

The conversion ritual normally includes immersion in a *mikvah* (the ritual bath); a meeting with a panel of three rabbis, known as a *bet din;* and an actual or ceremonial circumcision for men (see "Let's Go to a Circumcision!"). The person converting must indicate to the bet din panel the desire to fulfill the responsibilities and obligations of being a Jew as well as the willingness to give up those aspects of the former faith that are contrary to Judaism. While there are always exceptions, those are the steps typically taken in the conversion process.

Some conversions place a great emphasis on the study of Jewish knowledge, history, and those factors that make a person a Jew. It is not unusual for converts to wind up having a greater knowledge of what Judaism is all about than many people who were born into it.

Orthodox rabbis (including the official rabbinate of the State of Israel) do not accept conversions performed by non-Orthodox rabbis for a number of reasons. The entire subject of conversion to Judaism and who is considered a Jew and who is not can be a source of friction, especially outside of the United States.

I have a good friend who is Jewish. He married a woman who is a convert to Judaism. She considers herself Jewish; her friends and family consider her Jewish. While she was pregnant with their first son, they were living in Germany, where my friend was studying at the University of Heidelberg. After the child's birth, my friend and his wife sought to have him circumcised, but discovered that the Orthodox rabbi in Germany would not perform the ritual. Because the mother was converted by a non-Orthodox American rabbi, she was not recognized as a Jew by the German rabbinate, all of whom are Orthodox. Being resourceful, my friend and his wife took the child and slipped across the border to France, where a French rabbi performed the brit. It's a good story, but it illustrates an area of conflict within Judaism. (I remember hearing of an incident in which parents were able to have their son circumcised in Germany when they were denied the ritual in France!)

Often people who seek conversion to Judaism do so because they plan to marry someone of the Jewish faith. They wish to share this aspect of family life with their partner and raise children in a home with a single religion. Of course, converting to a new religion does not immediately make you into something new. The process takes time as the convert adjusts to a new way of life. The family of the convert—parents, children, siblings, cousins, and distant relatives—may be surprised or even shocked at the decision and may not know how to react when they meet the newly converted Jew: "Does this mean you can't eat bacon anymore?" "Does this mean I give you a present at Hanukkah instead of Christmas?" "Are you allowed to give *me* a Christmas gift?"

There will be other stressful times. How does a person who is now Jewish worship at the Christian funeral service of a deceased family member or friend? What about Christmas dinners, parties, cards, and gifts? What about Santa?

Conversion to Judaism isn't always smooth sailing. However, after much study, research, dialogue, and soul-searching, a person who converts to Judaism generally finds what he or she desires.

Intermarriage

These days, many Jews marry non-Jews. If the couple plans a nonreligious wedding service, there will be no difficulty in getting married as far as religion is concerned. If the couple desires a Jewish marriage ceremony, they can usually locate a rabbi who will perform the religious marriage service. However, many (if not most) rabbis refuse to conduct marriage ceremonies between a Jew and a non-Jew. Why?

An interreligious union contradicts the purpose of a Jewish marriage service—the joining of a Jewish bride and groom who are committed to sharing a Jewish home and raising in the Jewish tradition any children they might have or adopt. Such a marriage can often contradict the purpose of the non-Jewish partner's religion as well.

At the Jewish wedding ceremony, as the groom places the ring on the bride's finger, he will say, "You are consecrated to me according to the laws of Moses and Israel." If one member of the couple is not Jewish, is he or she truly being consecrated unto the other according to the laws of Moses and Israel?

As you might imagine, one of the principle Jewish objections to intermarriage is that it causes an eventual loss of Jewish identity and religiosity in the family, resulting in the further diminishing of an already small group of people.

Throughout my life, I have met many couples who have intermarried. Some of these couples have wonderful marriages, and others do not. I have also seen the divorce and breakup of many couples, both Jewish and intermarried. Being a Jewish couple certainly does not prevent this.

The children born to some intermarried couples receive a Jewish upbringing, but others do not. Sometimes one parent cares more about religion than the other, and this is how the decision is often made. Children exposed to the religions of both parents may wind up confused about their religious identity or may reject both. While attempting to identify with more than one religion may work for some people, others may come to a spiritual crossroads that presents major difficulties.

Some children who are brought up with no particularly strong religious background "find religion" later in life and become steeped in their newly discovered traditions. This happened to a very good friend of mine. His father was an Irish Catholic, and my friend was raised as Catholic. He has an Irish surname. He went to Catholic schools and even attended Catholic universities. His mother was a totally nonobservant Jew. At some point in his adult life, he chose to pursue Judaism. A conversion ceremony was not necessary because he was born to a Jewish mother.

Even with his Irish name and Catholic upbringing and education, he is considered as much a Jew as I am (who was born of two Jewish parents, attended Hebrew school for what seemed like a hundred years, and had a bar mitzvah at age thirteen). My friend is one of those rarities—a born-again Jew.

Many intermarried couples are angry that their respective religions (particularly Judaism and Catholicism) appear to be against their unions. One friend told me that "it was practically impossible" to find a rabbi who would marry her to her non-Jewish partner.

I know of another couple whose marriage was officiated by both a priest and a rabbi. Many guests thought that this was the neatest thing in the world, and the bride and groom have become another in the legion of couples who have a Christmas tree and a Hanukkah menorah side by side in their living room. This may seem to be a perfect union of the religions, but a basic question must be considered: under these circumstances, can each partner, as well as the children of the union, pursue the true nature of either religion?

The world of religion is a complex one, and it goes beyond mere ritual and tradition to the essence of belief in God and the source of creation and the universe. Most often, the spiritual side of marriage is given less thought than the "love" side, and the desire for a religious ceremony may be based more on tradition and the wishes of the couple's parents.

No one knows at the time of the marriage how such decisions will affect the future of the relationship and the children born of that relationship. It remains to be seen. There is obviously a lot more to consider when contemplating an interreligious marriage than whether or not to have a rabbi officiate.

Marriage, family, and religion are very, very complicated issues, aren't they?

Much information about intermarriage can be obtained from the outreach movements associated with the Reform and Conservative Jewish movements. Experienced counselors who are familiar with all types of interreligious situations and problems can be contacted through any synagogue or local Jewish Family and Children's Service office.

Religious Apparel and Dress

Except for a few ritual garments worn only during religious worship, most American Jews today do not dress in any special way. However, there are certainly clothing customs and traditions to which more observant Jews adhere.

Often you will see a Jewish man wearing a skullcap, sometimes held to the back of the head with a hairpin. This is called a *kippah* (Hebrew) or *yarmulke* (Yiddish). It has been a Jewish custom (not a law) for countless generations for males to cover their heads, symbolizing submission to God. Generally, any man or woman approaching the ark containing the Torah has his or her head covered. Some wear the kippah only during religious services, others wear the kippah when eating or during the study of Torah, and still others wear them always.

Reform Jews rejected the covering of the head for many years, but traditions and rituals sometimes return. These days many Reform congregants, both men and women, wear *kippot* (plural) during services or when in the synagogue.

I find it interesting that Christian clergy, including the pope, often wear a silk skullcap similar to the kippah or yarmulke worn by Jews. The cap, known as a *zucchetto* or *pileolus,* may have originated in the very early Church as the covering of the clerical tonsure, and it is seen in paintings from the thirteenth century. Different colors were used by the various ranks of the hierarchy during the Middle Ages and early Renaissance. Although there is some question of whether the kippah and the zucchetto are related, they are very similar.

A tallit is a ritual prayer shawl. *Tallitot* (plural) come in many sizes, colors, and styles, and are worn during religious services. In Numbers 15:38, the Lord instructed Moses to tell the Israelite people to "make fringes on the corners of their garments...and to put a blue cord on the fringe at each corner" (see "An Invitation to a Bar Mitzvah and a Bat Mitzvah"). These fringes are called *tzitzit.*

While Hasidic Jews and many other religious Jews wear garments containing tzitzit under their outer clothing, most contemporary Jews wear a tallit, which incorporates the tzitzit, only while praying in the synagogue or at special religious occasions (Orthodox Jewish women, by tradition, do not wear a tallit). The tzitzit serve to remind the wearer to observe all the commandments of the Torah.

Christian churchgoers know that priests and ministers of various denominations wear a garment that looks very much like a tallit. This vestment, the stole, often has fringes, and is worn at liturgical functions. Once again, some observers question whether the stole evolved from the Jewish prayer garment. However, it is certainly reminiscent of the tallit, as described in Numbers 15:38.

The tallit and kippah have become not only fashion items but also works of art. My niece wore a pink tallit at her bat mitzvah, and my son and I wore matching royal blue silk tallit and kippah sets for his bar mitzvah. Prayer shawls may be made of hand-painted silk or feature beautiful embroidery. A tallit can be reminiscent of Chagall's stained-glass windows or a desert scene. I have a kippah that features musical notes, and I've seen others made of all kinds of materials displaying yellow happy faces, sports themes, American flags, dinosaurs—you name it. The design is secondary to the function, obviously.

If you were to attend weekday morning religious services in an Orthodox or Conservative synagogue or view drawings or paintings of religious Jews in prayer, you would note that some of the congregants wear two small black boxes—one attached by a leather strap to the left arm and a second attached to the forehead. These items are called *tefillin*, or phylacteries, and the boxes contain parchment on which are written verses from the books of Exodus and Deuteronomy. The use of the tefillin is part of traditional prayer ritual.

A *kittel* is a white robe worn on special occasions. In the synagogue on major festivals such as Rosh Hashanah and Yom Kippur, a kittel may be worn by some congregants as well as the rabbi, the cantor, and the blower of the shofar. I recently attended Yom Kippur services at an Orthodox synagogue in France, and some members of the congregation were wearing kittel. It's fairly common for a bridegroom to wear a kittel at his wedding, and the leader of a Passover seder may choose to wear one. Often, the kittel is used as a burial shroud.

An interesting prohibition that comes directly from the Torah is that against wearing any clothing that contains a combination of wool and linen. Leviticus tells us, "You shall not let your animals breed with a different kind; you shall not sow your field with two kinds of seed; nor shall you put on a garment made of two different materials" (Leviticus 19:19). Whether the fibers are interwoven or pieces are sewn together or even if the linen is used as a "stiffener" in a collar or a liner in a jacket, it's just not permitted.

While walking in the ultra-Orthodox section of Jerusalem, I was surprised to see a notice posted on a telephone pole warning of a specific clothing product found to contain this prohibited textile combination (the warning was similar to the type we see in the newspapers informing us of a hazardous toy or an automobile recall).

Very observant Orthodox women do not wear pants or slacks, since this would be a violation of the biblical law that men should not wear women's clothing and vice versa (Deuteronomy 22:5). In addition to the ban on pants, women are required to be covered from the neck to the knee, with sleeves to the elbow, dark stockings (seamless stockings, which mimic "no stockings," may not be acceptable to some), and a hat, scarf, or wig that covers most or all of the hair. No bright colors are permitted, especially red, which is considered provocative.

This dress code may seem pretty severe, and by today's standards, it is. However, in certain sections of Jerusalem, signs are posted directing women to "dress modestly." While walking in one of these sections of the Holy City, I observed religious men averting their eyes and blocking their view with a hand as they passed women (generally tourists) who were not dressed in a manner the men considered appropriate. This included my wife, whom I thought was dressed appropriately for a walk in this neighborhood. She was wearing long sleeves, a head scarf, and a long skirt. I'm not sure what it was about her that was inconsistent with the "dress modestly" rule. Perhaps she's just naturally provocative.

Certainly the way you dress and carry yourself has a bearing on how the world views you. I am reminded of a story my cousin tells. His wife, who is not Jewish, always claimed that she didn't know any Jewish people when she was growing up—there were absolutely no Jews living in the small Southern town in which she lived.

After several years of marriage, my cousin happened to be glancing through a copy of the weekly hometown newspaper his wife subscribed to, and he noticed a story about a prominent citizen of the town, Rabbi Brown. The story featured a photo of a bearded man, who was pictured wearing glasses, a hat, and dark suit.

My cousin showed the photo to his wife. "I thought you told me there weren't any Jews where you grew up."

"Oh," she replied, "that's Rabbi Brown. He's not really a rabbi. Everyone just calls him that because he *looks* like a rabbi."

Hasidim and Hasidism

In the movie, *Annie Hall,* Alfie (Woody Allen) sits at the dinner table while Annie's family is eating a ham dinner. For a fleeting moment he is transformed into an ultrareligious Hasid, wearing the traditional garb of the nineteenth-century Jew—a large black hat, a long black frock coat, and a long beard with side-whiskers. People may think Allen is funny looking regardless of what he wears, but what is the significance of this outfit?

The Hasidim are generally considered an ultra-Orthodox sect within Judaism. The founder of modern Hasidism was Rabbi Israel ben Eliezer, born in 1698 in an area near the Polish–Russian border. Later given the honorary name Ba'al Shem Tov ("master of the good name"), he rebelled against formalized education and the academic foundation of religion and emphasized instead a simple, personal, pious spiritualism that was within the reach of all; anyone could pray to God, not only in a synagogue, but in any setting.

Spirited singing and dancing became part of the prayer and worship ritual, and Jewish mysticism in the form of the *Kabbalah* was popularized. Over the next two hundred years, the influence and teachings of Ba'al Shem Tov were spread to millions of Jews by his descendants and the descendants of his disciples.

The Hasidic movement is very patriarchal, and the leaders tend to be quite charismatic. Leadership is often passed down within families. Today, there are a number of Hasidic sects with names such as Bobover, Belzer, Satmar, Lubavitcher, Vishnitzer, Gerer, Klausenberger, Skverer, and Bratslaver. More than half of the Hasidim live in Israel, and the rest are scattered throughout the United States, Canada, Australia, Latin America, and European cities such as Antwerp, London, and Paris.

Hasidim maintain a strict separation between men and women who are not married to each other, not only in the synagogue, but in public and private as well. They believe that the mixing of the men and women in the synagogue would distract the men from their ritual prayer and study. As mentioned previously, Hasidic Jews would not attend a show or play featuring women on stage.

You may think it odd, but many if not most of the Hasidim refuse to accept the State of Israel as a political entity (although many live there). This refusal comes from their firm belief that until the coming of the Messiah, there can be no true Jewish state. While many describe themselves as anti-Israel, they are not anti-Israeli—a subtle but important difference.

Each Hasidic group wears a specific type of garb, generally black, which is reminiscent of Hasidism's eighteenth-century Eastern European roots; the differences in clothing styles are only identifiable by someone who follows this sort of thing. However, everyone intentionally dresses in this manner to set themselves apart from the mainstream Jewish and non-Jewish population (to the point of having buttons and buttonholes sewn on the side opposite from most men's clothing). The hair and sideburns of men and boys, as well as men's beards, are cut in a manner that can be traced to directives in Leviticus ("You shall not round off the hair on your temples or mar the edges of your beard" (Leviticus 19:27).

One Hasidic group (the Lubavitchers) maintains an outreach program in certain large cities where Jewish passersby are invited to say a few prayers or have a minicelebration of a current religious holiday. I have participated in this impromptu service on a couple of occasions, and I must report that it is not only a religious experience but somewhat of a mystical one as well. The men assisting in the ritual appear to be messengers from another era when my great-grandfathers may have dressed in a similar manner in some small, Eastern European shtetl.

While the Hasidim live and take part in the modern world, they are separated from the mainstream in many ways. Outside the home, they will eat only in kosher restaurants. They send their children to their own religious schools. Some of their customs would surprise an outsider. For example, a rule of modesty forbids an adult to be in the close physical presence of a stranger of the opposite sex for more than a short time. Even the shaking of hands or the hugging of close relatives or family members of the opposite sex is prohibited.

Not all of the Hasidim were born into this ultra-Orthodox group. Many thousands of young and/or disaffected Jews have returned to the faith over the past thirty years or so and comprise up to one-third of the Hasidim in the United States.

In addition to these converts, the ultra-Orthodox Hasidic population continues to grow as a result of their large families. Some people believe that within one hundred years this group could well represent the majority of the Jewish population.

No matter where they come from or what their beliefs, it is always interesting to see people dressed in an unusual manner. The Hasidim are not trying to make a fashion statement with the way they dress. However, I wonder if I might not personally feel more comfortable today wearing Hasidic garb than the leisure suit, half-buttoned, polyester, flowered shirt, gold neck chains, and platform heels that I wore during the mid-1970s.

Creation, Heaven, Hell, and Life after Death

Did God create the heavens, the seas, and every living thing on earth in six days? Is there an afterlife? Does Judaism believe in heaven and hell? After death are we punished for our sins and wrongdoing committed during life and rewarded for our good deeds?

These questions only spawn further questions, which reminds me of a riddle I learned as a teenager. One man asks another, "Why does a Jew always answer a question with a question?" The second man responds, "Why *shouldn't* a Jew answer a question with a question?"

Many modern Jews would agree that God created the universe; they also agree that this creation may be explained in scientific terms. Creation is an ongoing, ever-present process.

Was the Torah given to Moses on Mount Sinai, or was it revealed to the Jewish people in some other way? One answer to these questions might be that regardless of how the Jewish people received the Torah, we accept its guidance, wisdom, and teachings.

On the topic of life after death, Jewish concepts pertaining to this have changed through the ages and differ among the various branches of Judaism. So there are no agreed-on definitive responses I can offer.

What I can say is, Jews do not believe in the doctrine of original sin or the concept of salvation or of "being saved" as such; however, we do believe in transgression and redemption—the love and forgiveness of God. We believe in the concept of free will and recognize a difference between sins against other people and sins against God. To obtain forgiveness, we must seek it from those against whom we have transgressed.

The concept of hell as a place where the damned live is not firmly established in the Jewish tradition, nor is that of purgatory. Although there are references to Satan in certain scriptures, many Jewish people believe that Satan is no more than a symbol of the evil or negative temptations and impulses inside us all.

Throughout their history, Jews living in a particular society (Persian, Greek, or Christian, for example) have been influenced by the beliefs common to the majority population. These beliefs were also affected by how the Bible and other religious and scholarly writings were being taught and interpreted by contemporary religious leaders. Thus, there has been plenty of room for interpretation and personal belief when it comes to the devil and hell. These concepts, however, have not been central to Jewish tradition and scholarship.

Some Jewish authorities will say that we believe that the soul is eternal, and we will be rewarded for living a good life in the world to come. The Bible refers to a final resting place after death called Sheol. Defining or describing what Sheol is, however, is something that religious scholars have struggled with. While the concepts of reincarnation or the resurrection of the body have been popular in past centuries, especially during times of Jewish mysticism, these beliefs are not as popular today.

Parallel to the belief of an afterlife is the belief in the coming of the Messiah, who will usher in a time of peace, justice, and redemption. In addition, it is said that the Messiah will rebuild the destroyed temple, heal the sick, and fight the never-ending battle against evil. The concept of the Messiah, however, is also filled with speculation and interpretation. Some Jews believe not in a personal Messiah, but in a messianic age, a time of peace, justice, enlightenment, and kindness.

When I was growing up, I believed that after death we lived on in our good deeds and through our children. Contemporaries with similar religious backgrounds have expressed similar notions when I spoke to them about it. Unfortunately, I am not as sure about these things now as I was when I was a teenager and knew everything.

Where, When, and How Many

The history of the Jews is filled with many migrations as a result of expulsion, periodic changes in government and leadership, and the destruction of Jewish communities. For example, the Jews were expelled from the Holy Land in 586 BCE after the destruction of the First Temple and again in 70 CE after the destruction of the Second Temple. Later, because of religious persecution, Jewish people were expelled from England in 1290, from France in 1394, from Spain in 1492, and from Vienna in 1670. These expulsions caused great migrations of Jewish populations from one country to another.

In more recent times, political and religious persecution have made it difficult to determine the exact numbers of Jews in places such as the former Soviet Union since during these many years of persecution a great number of people lost their Jewish heritage.

Jews live all over the world, and some live in the most unlikely spots for the most unlikely reasons. One of my favorite stories is about a colleague's grandfather, who, when leaving Europe at the turn of the century, was trying to get to Chicago where he had family members. His English was poor, but he knew that Chicago was in the Midwest or, as he translated it, "the center of America." Instead of Chicago, he arrived in Central America and helped found the Jewish community in Costa Rica.

Jewish communities have existed in China, India, and other places where you might not expect that Jews would live, but these communities have dwindled or disappeared over the years.

Today, there are approximately thirteen million Jewish people living around the world. (When you consider that six million Jews perished under Nazi rule, you realize the impact of the Holocaust on the Jewish population.)

The first Jewish settlers to the American colonies came in 1654, and by 1900 the United States had almost a million Jewish inhabitants. Today, about half of the world's Jews live in the United States and Canada—2 percent of the population of the United States is Jewish. Of course, many Jews live in Israel, too, but Jewish people live almost everywhere—Russia, the Middle East, Africa, South America, Australia—you name it.

As a result of intermarriage, assimilation, and a declining birth-rate, the American Jewish population has not grown much. Except for one group—the ultra-Orthodox Hasidic population, discussed earlier.

Ashkenazic and Sephardic Jews

As if there weren't already enough differences and divisions among the Jews, there's still another. Through the Middle Ages and up until the Christian conquest of Spain and Portugal, the Jews living in these countries (called *Sephardim* or *Sephardic* Jews) had been living under Muslim rule. The Jews of Germany and Eastern Europe (called *Ashkenazim* or *Ashkenazic* Jews) did not have a Muslim influence. As a result, the two groups showed marked differences in Jewish custom, prayer, pronunciation of the Hebrew language, and other traditions linked to the societies and environments from which they had come.

In 1492 (while Christopher Columbus was sailing to the new world), Jews in Spain who refused to convert to Christianity were killed or sent into exile. Up to 100,000 Jews (a large number in those days) emigrated to the Near East and North Africa, joining existing Jewish communities and assimilating to the extent that many of the rites and customs of the Spanish Jews were adopted by the host communities. At the same time, the

Jews of Germany were quite numerous, and these Jews later migrated to other Eastern and Western European countries.

Besides differences in food, music, and religious writings, each group developed its own language. Yiddish, spoken by the Ashkenazim, is basically a combination of Hebrew and German, with other words from various regions thrown in. Ladino, spoken by the Sephardim, is a combination of Hebrew, Spanish, and Portuguese.

While there might be a few Ladino words that have crept into everyday usage, the number of Yiddish words bandied about by both Jews and non-Jews in conversation, films, and literature is extensive. Some of the many words that have found their way into common language usage include *maven, chutzpah, schlemiel, schlock, schmendrick, schmooze, kibitz, gonif, yenta, gelt,* and *shtick.*

Except for France, which has a large population of Sephardic immigrants from its former North African Arab colonies, most of the Jews of Europe and the West are Ashkenazic—up to 75 percent of the Jewish population. In Israel, however, more than 50 percent of the Jews are Sephardic, and people who speak Hebrew in Israel use the Sephardic pronunciation.

In Yemen and Ethiopia, there also are Jewish populations, both of which practiced their religion in relative isolation for many years. Their pronunciation of Hebrew as well as certain religious and cultural customs evolved in a quite different manner from those of other Jews. Periodically, other long-lost descendants of the Jewish people are identified living in remote areas of the world. While only fragments of their Jewish traditions may remain, these are often enough to identify them as Jews.

Through the years, the differences between the Sephardim and Ashkenazim have become blurred as people have adapted to the customs and cultures of their new homelands and as inter-marriage has occurred between members of the two groups. Many of the wonderful traditions of these two cultures live on, however, in the vast storehouse of folklore, fiction, humor, music, and wonderful food.

Women and Judaism

Judaism is a very old religion, established long before the terms "gender equality" and "politically correct" were in common usage.

The traditional role of Jewish women, as in many cultures, was in the home. The lighting of the Shabbat candles, welcoming Queen Sabbath into the home, is still considered a woman's rite; it is performed by a man only when a woman is not present. Through the ages, a child's Jewishness was determined by the mother—if the mother was Jewish, the child was Jewish. (Reform Judaism recognizes as Jewish the children of a Jewish father and a Gentile mother if the child is being raised as a Jew in a Jewish home.)

Today, women are ordained rabbis in the non-Orthodox movements and many serve as cantors. Although the lineage of the Jewish priesthood has been passed through males directly from Aaron, there are instances of female Kohanim performing

the priestly function at the High Holidays in some Conservative congregations that maintain this ritual (see "Jewish Priests").

On a more political note, the State of Israel can boast that it
is one of the few modern democratic countries that has had a
female leader (the late Prime Minister Golda Meir). Women
routinely serve as presidents and in other leadership roles in both
large and small religious congregations.

However, the story of women in Judaism is still being written. News articles and Web site postings abound with the stories of women attempting to achieve parity in the more orthodox
areas of Judaism; sometimes they achieve small victories, but
often they suffer frustrating setbacks.

Knowing as we do the patriarchal origins of Judaism, it is not
surprising that there is a (man's) prayer thanking God for "not
having created me a woman." One explanation for the existence
of this type of prayer is that because women traditionally are
exempt from certain religious obligations that men must perform, men consider themselves fortunate in that they are not
"relieved" of an opportunity to worship.

We must remember that much of the Talmud was written at
a time and in a place when women had little power and were
considered outsiders when it came to laws (including divorce
laws) that determined rights and privileges. In the synagogue,
women would sit apart from men, either in a balcony or behind
a curtain, where they would not be a "distraction" to the men
while they prayed. (Separation of the sexes is no longer the case
in modern, liberal congregations but is still the rule in Orthodox
synagogues, although the separation may be more a symbolic
than a physical barrier. A greater separation of the sexes occurs

in the more ultra-Orthodox and Hasidic congregations.)

While participating in Yom Kippur services in a large, Orthodox synagogue in France, I was sitting near a man who was deaf. Periodically during the service, he would use sign language to communicate with his wife who was sitting at least a hundred feet away in the women's balcony section (I had a feeling they were talking about their plans to break the fast and who would walk their children home). While the traditional purpose of separating men and women may have been to avoid distraction, there was virtually no barrier in this case despite the distance.

The Talmud tells a man to clothe himself according to his means but to clothe his wife above his means, and it is traditional to explain that God created the heaven, the earth, and all living things in an *ascending* order. As you remember, God's final creation was not man; it was woman.

Today, 50 percent of Reform rabbinical students are women. The number of female Conservative rabbis is increasing, and a greater number of female cantors add their voices to religious worship each year. I am pleased to say that my wife and I were married in a ceremony presided over by a female rabbi *and* a female cantor (see "To Reform . . .").

More and more I meet women who consider (and label) themselves Jewish feminists, many of whom participate in research, conferences, and study groups exploring both the historical and contemporary role of women in Judaism. These groups examine the symbols, rituals, and traditions of Jewish women, such as the *mikvah* (ceremonial bath), the bat mitzvah, and the holiday of Rosh Hodesh (the celebration of the new moon) in the light of modern life.

In recent years, Reform and Conservative congregations have rewritten religious services that once mentioned only the patriarchs of Judaism (Abraham, Isaac, and Jacob) to include the matriarchs (Sarah, Rebecca, Rachel, and Leah) as well. In Hebrew, God is now described not only using masculine terms but in feminine terms as well. *Shechinah,* the Hebrew word that describes God's divine presence, is used by many today to refer to God's feminine attributes or to the "female side" of God.

The struggle for gender equality is an old one. In the Torah, the daughters of Zelophehad petitioned Moses to gain the right to inherit what was their father's. The daughters asked why they should lose their father's inheritance just because he had no son. "The LORD spoke to Moses, saying: The daughters of Zelophehad are right in what they are saying" and granted them the inheritance (Numbers 27:6–7).

Thousands of years of tradition generally do not change dramatically overnight. However, in my own lifetime, I have seen significant changes take place in Judaism, and I foresee a continuation of this evolution with time.

Judaism
in the World

Israel

A visit to Israel is like a visit to no other place in the world. It is a mixture of the ancient and the modern, the religious and the secular, the familiar and the strange. Israel also is home to some of the most astounding archeological and historical sites in the world.

For many years I put off taking a trip to Israel. As were many other people, I was deterred by the seemingly endless threats of violence and terrorism. In fact, when you read these words, Israel may well be in the midst of a short- or long-term military action. Such has been the case from the very beginnings of the small nation.

In my own case, I finally realized that if I waited for newspaper headlines to declare "Peace in the Middle East," I might never get there in my lifetime. So I put my fears behind me and convinced my wife to do the same. We made our first "pilgrimage to the Holy Land" and proceeded to have the most wonderful experience imaginable.

In Israel, airport security is always at the highest level. Young soldiers of both sexes, generally armed, are everywhere. Military service is compulsory for both men and women. While it takes a little getting used to, all of this serves as a reminder to the visitor that even during times of "peace" the country stands on a military alert of some level. Soon, the soldiers become a natural part of the scenery.

After visiting several of the places on our itinerary, I began to see that despite the varying degrees of military alert, Israel has everything a visiting tourist could want. Its scenery includes both lovely and stark landscapes, and views of hills and desert. It has the Dead Sea, where tourists bob around in the water like corks or sit in natural hot springs at a spa. Israel has ancient villages, modern cities (including Tel Aviv), and archaeological ruins. There is the Mediterranean coast and the beach resort of Elat.

The harbor city of Haifa is home to the impressive Baha'i Temple, the Baha'i being one of many non-Jewish faiths present in Israel. The biblical cities of Bethlehem and Nazareth draw many Christian visitors on pilgrimage. One of my most vivid memories is of Bet She'an, the excavation site of a Roman-built city filled with amphitheaters, column-lined promenades, and splendid public and private structures. In the beautifully renovated area of Tel Aviv known as Jaffa is the site where Jonah set off on his voyage before being detained by the whale.

Each site in Israel—Akko (Acre), Caesarea (Horbat Qesari), Safed (Zefat), the caves near Qumran (where the Dead Sea Scrolls were found), the Golan Heights, the Sea of Galilee, Tiberias, and, of course, Masada (home to the fortress of Herod and the last stand of the Zealots)—offers a wealth of beauty and culture, intrigue and drama.

Then there is Jerusalem. As you stroll through the Jewish, Muslim, and Christian quarters of the Old City, you experience, with every one of your senses, thousands of years of history. Jerusalem elicits excitement, tension, and a heightened awareness that you have entered a holy place. If you haven't already been there, I hope that someday you can see it for yourself.

More than being a wonderful place to visit, Israel is first and foremost the Jewish homeland. Abraham, the first Jew, was told by God, "Go from your country and your kindred and your father's house to the land that I will show you. I will make of you a great nation" (Genesis 12:1–2). This one simple biblical statement forms the covenant between God and Israel, and this dream of the Jewish homeland has been kept alive for centuries. Through the ages, Jewish people have considered this covenant sacred, and regardless of how often they were expelled, exiled, enslaved, or faced with death, the symbol of the Jewish homeland remained alive in their dreams, hopes, prayers, and literature.

The truth of the matter is that throughout their history, the vast majority of Jews have lived in what is called the *Diaspora* (anyplace outside the land of Israel), and for only a short time in history did they have any real control over the region.

At the end of the nineteenth century, the desire for a Jewish homeland evolved as the political movement Zionism. This desire coincided with a new wave of anti-Semitism in Europe and czarist Russia. Plans for the extermination of the Russian Jews, the Dreyfus Affair in France (wherein a Jewish army

officer was falsely accused of a crime and sentenced in a sensa-
tional public trial), and anti-Semitic riots in Germany and elsewhere led the Zionists to begin thinking of the creation of a
Jewish state.

Certainly, Adolf Hitler's murder of six million Jews expedited
the creation of Israel, but the stage was set much earlier. Jewish
people believe that the land of Israel is sacred and holy. As a matter of fact, there is a traditional "hierarchy of holiness" that dates
back to the time of the temple. The holiest spot was the central
room in the temple sanctuary. This room, called the Holy of
Holies, was visited only once a year on Yom Kippur, the holiest
day of the year, and then only by the high priest. Surrounding
the Holy of Holies were other rooms within the temple, the
temple itself, the temple grounds, the city of Jerusalem, and then
the land of Israel—each room, each area, each region becomes
incrementally "less holy" as the distance from the central room
increased (see "The Temple").

Thus, you can see why Jews place so much importance on the
State of Israel as well as on the holy city of Jerusalem in particular. Many of the prayers said by Jews throughout the world contain the words, "Next year in Jerusalem" or "Pray for Jerusalem."
Throughout history, Jews evicted from Jerusalem during periodic military invasions considered themselves not living in their
new homeland but merely in a state of exile.

After the 1948 Arab-Israeli war, Jews were not permitted
access to the holy sites, but the Jewish people regained the city
after the 1967 Six-Day War. Following this war, desecrated sites
were renovated, and access again was provided to the Western
Wall (many people still refer to it as the Wailing Wall)—the only

remaining vestige of the First Temple. Much activity—religious, educational, mercantile, and tourist— takes place within the Old City today.

Much of the ongoing conflict involving Israelis, Palestinians, and other Arab neighbors revolves around the centuries-old argument about who is entitled to land in the Middle East—the families who live there, the country whose armies have fought and successfully captured it, the groups who claim it as their own because it is ordained in the Bible, and so forth. As I write this, lives continue to be lost because of these religious-political-military arguments. There is no greater oxymoron to me than the phrase "Peace in the Middle East."

Since the founding of the State of Israel, there has existed a Law of Return that gives every Jew the right to emigrate and relocate to Israel. Israel has accepted and absorbed wave after wave of immigrants—Holocaust survivors, Eastern Europeans, and Russians fleeing oppression, and thousands of Ethiopian Jews. Israel's founders declared Hebrew the official language, and the early settlers tackled the near-impossible task of reviving and expanding the all-but-dead language, which is now the common language spoken by all Israelis (a native-born Israeli is known as a *sabra*). These pioneers turned desert into farms and built new cities and settlements to house the waves of newcomers. Through the years, attempts to alter or revoke the Law of Return have not been successful.

Don't think for a minute that it is a simple or easy matter for a small nation about the size of New Jersey to absorb large numbers of immigrants. However, the people of Israel can never forget that through the centuries exiled Jews have wandered the land looking for a place to live, facing barriers, and being turned away by country after country, often perishing in the process.

Thus, the open-door policy welcoming all Jews to Israel remains in effect in spite of periodic political opposition from some corners. The law signifies that Jews need not fear having no place to go in the face of anti-Semitism and persecution.

The Jews in America and throughout the world provide a great amount of financial support for Israeli social, religious, educational, cultural, agricultural, and political organizations and programs. The list of groups giving and receiving aid is endless, reflecting the passionate and pragmatic support of the country by individuals and groups.

Early settlers in what was to become the State of Israel formed kibbutzim. Each kibbutz was set up as an agricultural cooperative; the living was difficult, uncomfortable, and often primitive. These settlers were idealists, willing to sacrifice personal comfort in an effort to make the goal of the kibbutz a reality.

As the State of Israel has become more viable economically and politically, life on the kibbutz has changed; the living is more comfortable, and the focus has expanded beyond agriculture to include manufacturing and tourism. For many years, a visit or extended stay on a kibbutz has been the goal of many American teenagers and young adults who subsequently never forget the role this visit played in their lives. Many Americans retire or semiretire in Israel.

Visitors to Israel may choose to study at an *ulpan*, an intensive language school where conversational Hebrew is taught. As part of a nine-month visit in Israel, my daughter studied

Hebrew, lived on a kibbutz and traveled extensively throughout the country.

The Hebrew date corresponding to May 15, 1948, marks the day when Israel became a sovereign state, and this is the date on which Israel Independence Day is celebrated in typical fashion with fireworks, parties, flags, and music. (The day is known as *Yom Ha-Atzma'ut* in Hebrew.)

While many people consider Israel a Jewish state, its government is not headed by a religious leader. Israel is a democracy with a parliament known as the Knesset, which consists of locally elected delegates, some of whom are Muslims or Christians. (Muslims and Christians also control and maintain their own religious sites.)

Israel is run in a manner similar to the British system, sporting a fair number of political parties as well as political blocs that can link up to vote for or against other parties. Thus, the balance of power shifts from the right to the left depending on many economic, political, social, and world issues. So what else is new?

While the Israeli government practices what we would call separation of church and state, there are many things that are affected by religious factions. For example, Christians and Muslims decide their own rules regarding marriage and funerals, and the Orthodox Jewish establishment decides on issues regarding Jewish marriages, funerals, dietary laws in public institutions, and the like. Public transportation is limited on Shabbat. Jewish marriages, divorces, and religious conversions are based on Orthodox practices rather than the Conservative or Reform practices common in the United States (causing certain problems and controversies not yet resolved). Kosher dietary laws are observed in the military and in government institutions.

There are small but growing Reform, Conservative, and Reconstructionist presences in Israel. However, Orthodox rabbis generally determine the religious character of life there. This influence certainly has an impact not only on the day-to-day living of the population but also on political aspects of the country. Clashes between the religious right and the more liberal, progressive elements find their way via the media to the American people, who can easily compare these conflicts to similar clashes in our own society.

Some opponents of Israel describe all Jews as Zionists, but this is simply not the truth. Many of the most ultra-Orthodox Jewish people in the world today are anti-Zionist, even to the point of objecting to the existence of the State of Israel and the use of Hebrew, the "holy tongue," as a spoken language.

I could go on and on, but suffice it to say that the whole subject of the State of Israel and the Israeli people, and Judaism and the Jewish people, is quite complicated. As it is in any democracy, Israel will change and evolve with time.

I hope and pray that there will come a time very soon when we can visit Israel and other places in the Middle East without fear. It is such a wonderful place.

Jewish Art and Music

When we speak of Jewish art and music, what do we mean? Do we refer to the chants or songs we recite or sing during a religious service? Do we refer to beautiful stained-glass windows that decorate a synagogue or the Marc Chagall windows in Jerusalem?

Do we include Leonard Bernstein's *Kaddish,* regularly performed by symphonies around the world? How about the music from *Fiddler on the Roof?* Is the local Jewish craftsperson who designs seder plates and *mezuzot* (plural of *mezuzah*) creating Jewish art?

If I speak of traditional Jewish music, sung in Hebrew by a cantor in a synagogue, does it matter that some of this "traditional" music may be only forty or eighty years old?

What about klezmer, a style of music currently enjoying a phenomenal revival in popularity? The word *klezmer,* which means "instruments of song" in Hebrew, was used to describe itinerant Jewish musicians in Eastern Europe after the Middle

Ages. By the nineteenth century, klezmer musicians had carved out a musical niche for themselves, playing folk tunes, waltzes, mazurkas, and other dance music at weddings, parades, and fairs for Jewish (and often Gentile) audiences.

Should klezmer music, which is based on Polish, Hungarian, and Romanian folk tunes and the Jewish musical repertoire of *freylekhs, sher,* and *khosidl* tunes, be considered Jewish music? Like many questions regarding things Jewish, this one only spawns more questions.

I would suggest that there are three types of Jewish art and music. The first comes out of antiquity and was integral to Jewish religious service and life. Little of this art and music still exists, although there is evidence of it. We know that in ancient times, religious services in the temple were accompanied by an orchestra, although songs from this period are lost. Medieval religious books were often decorated in color and gold leaf, and some of these survive. The discovery and restoration of ancient synagogues and other holy sites in Israel have revealed mosaics, wall and ceiling paintings, and decorations of wood, ceramics, and metal.

The second category is songs and art from the past few hundred years. We have singers of Ladino Jewish music who give concerts in that language and revivals of Yiddish music and musical plays from the turn of the century. Many beautiful tapestries and Torah covers and crowns are displayed in museums around the world.

The third category is contemporary Jewish art and music. An abundance of wonderful Judaica is produced today in all types of media, from ceramic to gold and silver, cloth, wood, and so on. Synagogues are decorated inside and out with all kinds of art and artwork.

Jewish composers continue to write large orchestral pieces as well as simple musicals and folk songs. Often this music finds its way into the religious service and liturgy, and because of the power of the mass media, a song like "Sunrise, Sunset" can become a standard, performed regularly at family affairs and functions. There are rock groups and rap singers who perform new Jewish works in both English and Hebrew. Some of these songs are based on old melodies but many use contemporary sounds, and new Jewish holiday songs are written all the time.

Every culture values its artists and musicians, and the Jewish culture is no different. A painting, a weaving, a sculpture, and even a song based on a religious subject or holiday is, to me, more than a work of art. It can be, and often is, a symbol or reflection of the spiritual side of life.

By the way, if you don't like rock or rap music in English, you probably won't care for the Hebrew versions, either.

Mysticism and the
Repair of the World

What would a great religion be if it did not have deep secrets and mysterious happenings? *Kabbalah* gives all this and more to Judaism. When a Spanish Jew named Moses de Leon discovered a book called the *Zohar* ("Illumination") at the end of the thirteenth century, each letter, syllable, and word of the Torah was endowed with a secret as well as literal meaning. Hidden spiritual messages and the secrets of creation could be found, it was said, by carefully examining the biblical text. (Warning: there are many scholars who questioned the book's authenticity then as well as today.)

The Kabbalists believed that during the process of creation something went wrong—the light that God exhaled was too strong for the vessels meant to hold it, and as a result the sparks of God's light were scattered throughout the world. They believe that these hidden sparks are everywhere and that it is only by understanding the mystical forces and performing mitzvot (following the commandments and doing good deeds) that the world would ultimately be repaired.

Tikkun olam, the reparation of the world, is today the primary goal and ultimate responsibility of many Jews. The method of this repair takes different forms. Traditionally, performing mitzvot and following the commandments, rules, and customs set down through the centuries was believed to be the way. Contemporary interpretation, however, includes more social, political, and not exclusively Jewish activities—working for peace, helping to clean up the environment, and fighting for equality and an end to bigotry and injustice. Certainly, tikkun olam is a tall order, and what started as a mystical concept can be (and has become for many) a way of life.

An item of interest: almost every mention of Kabbalah in books on Judaism contains a footnote that many European Christians were, at one time, interested in Jewish mysticism and that Catherine the Great of Russia wished to learn Hebrew so that she could read Kabbalah. I have not discovered if Catherine ever got past her Hebrew ABC's.

Since its introduction centuries ago, Kabbalah has had its advocates and its detractors. It has also produced many scholars, some of whom have contributed much to the liturgy, philosophy, literature, and wisdom of the religion. Like other mystical traditions, Kabbalah seems always to have a life of its own. In fact, I'm not surprised to hear that Kabbalah is attracting attention from some unusual sources these days, including at least one well-known pop culture icon/actress/singer who might even be an ardent admirer of Catherine the Great.

Money—Stereotypes, Charity, and the Scriptures

During the Middle Ages, the Catholic Church prohibited the lending of money at interest, but this policy could be enforced only against Christians lending money to other Christians. It was at this time that Jews became associated with money lending, since they were one of the few non-Christian groups capable of coming up with sufficient funds to finance building projects, housing, and business and trade ventures. Very often Jews were invited to cities for the specific purpose of providing funding for the building of church and civic projects.

These were times during which Jews were separated from the rest of society by their lifestyle and dress. As a result, many careers and job opportunities were closed to them (it is only within recent generations that the Jewish people have lived among the general population as they do today). Jews were also prohibited from owning land. Money lending, even riskier then than it is today, was one of the few viable ways for a Jew to make a living.

Shakespeare popularized the negative stereotype of miserly or greedy Jews such as Shylock, and unfortunately this concept is a strong one that lives on in literature. History reveals that non-Jewish moneylenders, including the Italian banks, charged higher rates than the Jewish moneylenders did.

There are numerous examples in the Scriptures of lending money, paying debts, and offering fair compensation for goods, services, and damages. Interpretations of and teachings about these subjects advise us not only about the lending of money but about the giving of charitable contributions as well. It is from these teachings that we learn the importance of helping establish the recipients of loans in their own, self-sustaining businesses or trades, as well as the value of giving to charity anonymously. Moses Maimonides, a great twelfth-century rabbi, scholar, philosopher, and physician, enumerated the levels of charitable giving, starting with anonymous gifts that provide the means of self-sustenance, all the way to donations that are given without really wanting to. He was an advocate of the concept of tithing, recommending 10 percent of a person's income as a guideline for giving. Today's guidelines vary, but "giving" remains a common theme.

The Rabbis tell us that we are responsible for feeding the poor, both non-Jewish and Jewish, and the Talmud advises that even if we are on welfare we must give to the poor. It also tells us that *tzedakah,* which denotes the obligation of giving charitable donations in a cheerful and generous manner, is as important as all the other commandments combined. Before lighting the Sabbath candles, many families begin Shabbat with tzedakah ("coins"), a small gift to charity. (Generations of Jews are familiar with the small blue metal box in which tzedakah were deposited on a regular basis.) A portion of the costs of a celebration such as a bar or bat mitzvah or a wedding is often donated to charitable organizations. Whether a person is a philanthropist or just donates a few dollars whenever possible, tzedakah starts at home and is an inherent part of the Judaic tradition.

On the subject of donations, what could be more valuable than donating your time? In Judaism there is a centuries-old concept called *gemilut hasadim.* This tradition, which is described in the Talmud, defines acts of goodwill toward others and ranks these good deeds higher than mere contributions of money, since they require the actual involvement of the giver. Traditionally, there were six types of acts that fell into this category of good deeds: visiting the ill, providing clothing for the needy, giving comfort to mourners, accompanying the dead to their graves, being hospitable to strangers, and (on a happier side) giving assistance to brides.

Jews do not send flowers to a funeral (see "The High Holidays—Rosh Hashanah and Yom Kippur" and "A Jewish Funeral—Saying Good-bye to Uncle Harry"). In lieu of sending flowers, it has become a modern custom to make a donation to a charity either of the donor's choosing or designated by the family of the deceased.

Today, other activities have been added to broaden this list. Almost any volunteer activity in which you personally contribute your time and energy in helping the poor, the hungry, the disabled, the homeless, the sick, or the aged falls into this category. Any attempt to help repair or improve the environment counts.

Volunteering to teach English to immigrants, helping at animal shelters, or a million other things you can think of fall into the category of gemilut hasadim. This includes any assistance you may give to a bride.

Perform a Mitzvah

The word *mitzvah* (the plural is *mitzvot*) is a common word used when writing about things Jewish. It literally means "commandment"; however, it is commonly understood to mean "a good deed."

The terms *bar mitzvah* and *bat mitzvah* mean "the son" or "the daughter" of the commandment, in that the child is now ready to take the responsibility to understand the meaning and practice of mitzvot.

In speaking of performing a mitzvah, we refer to the performance of deeds that would please God, that make us feel joy, and that benefit ourselves, others, and the world. A mitzvah can be an act of charity and compassion or the simple act of saying a prayer before eating. It is in performing mitzvot every day, every month, and every year, year after year, that the true meaning of Judaism is found.

The Rabbis tell us that mitzvot must not be performed out of a sense of duty but rather for their own sake and without unnecessary harm to yourself, since you also have an obligation to enjoy your life.

Controversial Social Issues

When dealing with controversial issues such as abortion, capital punishment, birth control, suicide, homosexuality (and, for that matter, sexuality itself), Judaism looks at religious traditions surrounding the issue and then it looks at the facts, the evidence, and all sides of the story before coming to any conclusion. In the end, there really is no one conclusion.

While traditional or ultra-Orthodox Jews may cite a verse in an attempt to convince that the Bible or the Talmud tells us one thing, Conservative, Reform, and more liberal Jews can frequently quote another verse or give an example from later interpretations of the first verse that will result in a convincing argument that the opposite view is true, acceptable, or at least debatable.

From this, I come to the conclusion that—with the exception of certain crimes such as sexual assault, murder, and the prohibitions listed in the Ten Commandments—modern liberal

Judaism emphasizes free choice in decision making when it comes to many if not most moral and personal issues.

On the issue of birth control, you can read in the Talmud of situations in which women used birth-control methods centuries ago for reasons of physical and mental health. In situations when having more children would cause a mother undue stress or prevent her from adequately caring for her existing children, birth control was an acceptable practice. Today, family planning is not condemned by most modern rabbis and is certainly acceptable when the mother's life could be endangered by pregnancy.

The subject of abortion continues to be divisive both socially and politically in the United States and elsewhere. Jews believe that the life of the mother is more important than the life of the unborn child. During the Nazi reign, rabbis issued a ruling permitting abortions, since pregnant Jewish women were to be killed.

However, the unborn Jewish child has traditionally been afforded much respect. In fact, the Talmud says that during pregnancy the fetus is believed to study the Torah (sonograms have not yet confirmed this belief). While the fetus may have rights, the endangerment of the life of the mother, her mental health, and the well-being of her partner and her other children are taken into consideration. Thus, Judaism considers not only the life of the fetus but also the life of the entire family.

Within Judaism, there are proponents and opponents of both birth control and abortion, but neither is necessarily forbidden; each issue is examined within the framework of the situation and the persons involved.

Speaking of sex . . . In general, Judaism does not equate sex with either sin or amorality, but the ban on adultery does rank with the other nine commandments. (Note: in the Jewish numbering of the commandments, the adultery commandment is number seven, right after Thou Shall Not Murder and before Thou Shall Not Steal; Christians number the Ten Commandments in a slightly different way.) The Talmud, while prohibiting extramarital sex, does not place the same emphasis on premarital sex.

Judaism acknowledges the importance of sexual relations within a marriage. The lack of sex in a marriage and the withholding of sex from a spouse were traditionally grounds for divorce. It may be interesting to note that Shabbat became a customary time (although not necessarily the *only* time) for married couples to celebrate love and companionship and perform a mitzvah by having sexual relations.

The issue of Jewish gays and lesbians is a good example of how Judaism balances biblical pronouncements with contemporary trends and updated scientific and social research. In biblical times, homosexuality was considered "an abomination." While there will always be those who condemn lifestyles that are different from their own (which they consider the "normal" lifestyle), modern liberal Jewish thinking tends to accept a person's sexual preference and not consider it either moral or immoral.

In many large cities, there are active Jewish congregations predominantly made up of gay and lesbian Jews. In addition, gay and lesbian rabbis and cantors serve in a number of synagogues. Gay and lesbian Jewish couples very often form family units that include children.

So, while it is important to note that traditional Orthodox Judaism may not condone these views, there is certainly a place within the more liberal Jewish religious communities for alternative lifestyles. To me, this is simply further evidence that, as ancient a religion as it is, Judaism continues to be open to change and sensitive to new interpretations and insights.

Those people in favor of capital punishment will surely cite the verses, "If any harm follows, then you shall give life for life, eye for eye, tooth for tooth" (Exodus 21:23–24), and remind us that the Bible also tells us that "the murderer shall be put to death" (Numbers 35:18). However, as it is with many controversial issues, it's just not that simple.

The Talmud sets forth one safeguard after another to assure that a condemned person is not executed for a crime that he or she may not have committed. Complicated legal loopholes predating those of today were in place in Jewish courts long ago in an effort to place barriers against the use of capital punishment. (Please do not interpret this to mean that all Jews are against capital punishment; this is not the case.)

What of euthanasia, or physician-assisted death? Actively causing a person's death is not acceptable under Jewish law, but neither does this law require that intravenous feeding, for example, continue to be used on a terminally ill and horribly suffering patient.

The same logic holds in the case of suicide. While traditional Judaism condemns suicide to the point of prohibiting the suicide victim from being buried with customary religious services in the main section of a Jewish cemetery, this dishonor is usually avoided by assuming that it may not have been suicide (in the intentional sense) after all, but a period of mental illness, an accident, or who knows what.

When it comes to controversial social issues, Judaism tends to examine and weigh all sides and viewpoints very carefully. Historical Jewish law and commentary illustrate this over and over.

Old Wars and New Wars

The Bible is filled with stories of great wars and great warriors. In each case, the Israelite people rise up against tyrants or defend themselves against overwhelming odds. In Jewish legends, massacres, martyrs, and heroes abound.

What does Judaism believe about modern-day wars? History shows that Jews were conscripted into the armies of the czars and have fought in all American wars, including the Revolutionary and the Civil Wars. Jewish teachings advise us to follow the law of the land, and this must include defending one's country. While the Ten Commandments forbid murder, the Talmud advises that self-defense is not murder and that a war can be just.

Since its inception, the State of Israel has been involved in continual wars with its neighbors, interspersed with tense periods of peace. Israel has been portrayed alternately as the heroic defender of its little state and as the ignoble aggressor that uses its advanced military machinery to destroy its helpless enemy. Somewhere between these two extremes lies the truth.

Or perhaps, as is the case of the United States, sometimes a country is more justified in its actions than at other times; but only history and time will tell.

Judaism believes in the concept of the conscientious objector and allows for people to be exempt from military duty if they are "too 'tender' to serve," a phrase that can be interpreted in various ways. In addition, the Talmud tells us that a person fighting what he or she may consider an unjust war or fighting for an unjust government must obey his or her conscience first.

As anyone who visits Israel will affirm, in many ways the Jewish state is always on military alert. Virtually every Israeli citizen, male and female, serves in the military and serves many years in the reserves. This situation is not bound to change in the near future.

In spite of this ongoing military presence, I believe that not only the Jews of Israel, but the Jews throughout the world pray for peace—shalom—as much if not more than any other people.

The word *shalom* appears as the last word of many Jewish prayers, and its etymology is interesting. The English word *peace* comes from the Latin word *pax*, which means "quiet." *Shalom*, however, is derived from the Hebrew word *shalem*, which means "complete"; this is a subtle but significant difference.

Peace does not seem to come easily or without bloodshed in the Middle East. However, for the Jewish people, peace has been the goal for thousands of years.

The Chosen People

For you are a people holy to the Lord your God; the Lord your God has chosen you out of all the peoples on earth to be his people, his treasured possession.
(Deuteronomy 7:6)

Be careful what you wish for. Through history, being the "Chosen People" has led to all kinds of problems. For what, exactly, were the Jews chosen? Another in a string of good questions.

Some people believe that the Jews were given the mission to bring monotheism—the concept of the one omnipotent God—to all humanity. Others believe that the Jews were chosen to receive the Torah, the word of God. Still others believe they were chosen to serve God and were given the privilege of carrying the message of God through history, as Jewish people have done for the past three thousand years. With privilege comes responsibility.

The Talmud tells us that seven laws were given to Adam and passed down to Noah before Moses received the Ten

Commandments on Mount Sinai. These laws are referred to as the Seven Noahide Laws (or Commandments) and are considered a covenant between God and all the peoples of the world:

- To believe in the one God.
- Not to blaspheme.
- Not to kill.
- Not to steal.
- Not to be sexually immoral.
- To set up courts of law.
- Not to eat the flesh cut from an animal while that animal was still alive.

These laws required of "all humanity" seem reasonable and logical. The Jewish people, however, were given 613 commandments in the Torah. Many of these 613 commandments are applicable only to certain people within the religion, and some are no longer operative as a result of the destruction of the temple. Thus, no single Jew is currently responsible for fulfilling every one of the 613 commandments. This is a relief.

Anti-Semitism

Many, if not most, people have experienced discrimination in one form or another. Race, gender, sexual preferences, age, height, weight, disability, education, religion, country of origin, style of dress, and even personal beliefs can lead to exclusion, antagonism, discrimination, and, in some circumstances, hatred. Laws against this type of behavior help, but they cannot eradicate the feelings of others.

Because of their religious beliefs, Jews have been singled out over the millennia for persecution, violence, and slavery. Through the ages, forced conversions, prohibitions against the practice of Judaism, and laws specifically forbidding the study and teaching of the Torah have been commonplace. The incidence of pogroms, mass executions, deportations, expulsions, and individual acts of violence and terror are threaded throughout the fabric of the history of the Jews. The Crusades were a particularly terrible time for European Jews, many of whom were murdered during the onslaught of religious fervor. Stereotypes of miserly or wicked Jews live on in the literature of William Shakespeare, Charles Dickens, and many others.

I would venture that there is not a Jew alive today who has not heard, felt, or been the subject of some type of anti-Semitic comment, attack, joke, or slur. In a period of a week or two, it was not difficult for me to find examples of anti-Semitic behavior in the news:

- An anti-Semitic remark was scrawled in red ink on a grease board that a Jewish coach was to use in a talk to his college basketball team prior to a game. It read, "get ready for an ass-kicking, you Jew bastard." In a post-game interview, the coach said, "There's something a lot more important than basketball, all right? That's life and being a good person." An administrator from the opposing team's school said that the Jewish coach had impugned the school and the school's state in his reaction to the incident. Apologies on both sides continued for days.

- A book review of a former neo-Nazi's memoir tells of the members of an East German group devoted to Holocaust denial. The author reports that one group member has a yellow Star of David (a symbol that Nazis forced German Jews and those incarcerated in concentration camps to wear) inlaid in his toilet bowl. He also told of other members who cultivate "sadistic nostalgia" for concentration camp tortures. (Ironically, it is against German law to print or publish neo-Nazi literature in Germany.

Much of the printing of these documents is done in the United States.)

Over the following weeks and months, other stories appeared in the papers or came to my attention:

- A bottle is thrown through a synagogue window.
- Several car bombs explode in Israel.
- The Anti-Defamation League reports increases in the incidences of hate crimes against Jews in the United States.
- One of my patients insists on telling me a Jewish joke that turns out to be a slur.
- A friend of mine buying a car is accused by the salesman of trying to "Jew down" the price.
- A California physician and professor who lost twenty-five relatives during the Holocaust continues to push German authorities to investigate and prosecute a German doctor who allegedly led disabled children to death in a World War II Nazi "healing center" outside Dachau (Simon Wiesenthal, the famous Jewish Nazi hunter, has kept a file on this particular doctor, documenting his membership in the Nazi party and the SS and his work on Jewish and non-Jewish inmates in the Dachau clinic).
- Vandals break the front window of a Jewish family's home in order to destroy a lighted Hanukkah menorah.

- The FBI reports rumors of the plans of an extremist
  group to execute twelve hundred Jewish American
  business and professional people if the group's
  demands are not met.
- Police investigate the desecration of forty-three
  graves at a Jewish cemetery in a city located at the
  site of Auschwitz, the former Nazi death camp.

You don't have to look very far to find these and other stories. Anti-Semitism, neo-Nazism, religious hate crimes, and the popularization of individuals who promote anti-Jewish propaganda are ever-present factors. As this book goes to press, alarm is growing amongst Jews over the surge of anti-Semitic attacks in Europe and elsewhere in the world.

There are many places in the world today where Jews continue to be persecuted, prevented from obtaining particular jobs, imprisoned, and worse; this antagonism is directed toward non-religious as well as religious Jews.

Anti-Semitism is not just an act of violence or hatred. It is not just a physical attack on a building or a person. It is not just an organized plan to persecute a group of people. Anti-Semitism is the insidious and chronic hatred of and harmful actions against Jews by the ignorant and misinformed. Hatred of the Jews and the actions perpetrated against them occur for any number of reasons. But whatever the reason, we must continue to work towards increasing acceptance and tolerance of minorities in our society, including minority religious groups.

Keeping Judaism and the Jewish people alive has never been a simple task.

The Holocaust

During a trip to Hawaii a while ago, I came face-to-face with something I hadn't experienced in many years. While lying on a chaise at the pool, thinking about how great it was to leave my problems thousands of miles away, a man walked by and jolted me out of my reverie. Tattooed on his arm was the row of numbers found only on survivors of a Nazi concentration camp. I have never stopped thinking about this man, who was probably a teenager when he became a victim of modern history's greatest example of man's inhumanity to man.

The Holocaust is a painful topic, but it is one that cannot be ignored or avoided. To understand fully how the Holocaust could occur, it is helpful to know how and why Hitler and the Nazis came to power.

A number of years ago, I visited a friend whose young brother was writing a high school history paper. The title of his report was "The Causes of World War II." "What *were* the causes of World War II?" I asked. He paused for a moment and gave me a provocative answer: "I would say that World War II was mostly a result of the peace settlement of World War I."

German and world history scholars continue to debate the rise of Nazism, the causes of World War II, and the widespread racism and anti-Semitism of the period. However, one of the most accepted explanations has to do with the political and nationalistic discontent in Germany surrounding the Versailles Treaty and its aftermath—in short, the peace settlement of World War I.

After the German empire's defeat in World War I, it collapsed. The Versailles Treaty outlined the terms of peace in Europe. Although representatives of Germany had no part in drafting the document, they were forced to sign it. As a result, Germany was forced to accept sole responsibility for the war. It was also obligated to pay all costs of civilian damage resulting from the war.

German nationalists came to blame the new government for the poor state of affairs in which the country found itself. In the Reichstag (Parliament), no political party was able to achieve a majority, and therefore the government comprised a combination of several parties.

Just about everyone in Germany was unhappy and opposed the government. The middle class had lost everything as a result of inflation in the 1920s. Many unemployed workers, business owners, and landowners longed for a return to autocratic leadership.

Of the many political parties formed, one was the National Socialist German Workers Party, or the Nazis. The party appealed not only to criminals and outcasts, but to unemployed workers, demobilized soldiers, and youthful idealists as well. The party also appealed to property owners and businessmen who feared the loss of their property were the Communists to take control.

The Nazis promised to restore power to Germany by establishing a totalitarian state, redistributing national wealth, and creating jobs for everyone; they had the strong appeal of Nationalism and Socialism. In 1921, Adolf Hitler became the leader (führer) of the party.

Hitler had the ability to arouse crowds to hysteria. He was a fanatic who blamed Germany's decline in power on the Jews, and his most violent racial attacks were directed against them. Hitler espoused the concept that the Germans, as "Aryans," were members of a master race meant to rule the world. He believed that democracy and socialism were Jewish plots to destroy the Aryan race. Hitler's plan was to carve out an empire in Poland and Russia where the Aryan race could reside. He believed that the Slavic inhabitants of the land were inhuman and fit only to be slaves.

At first, the Nazis were prominent only in Southern Germany (Bavaria), and during the prosperous mid- and late 1920s most Germans did not take them seriously. However, with the onset of worldwide economic depression in 1929, more Germans began listening to Hitler, who was able to simplify complex issues and promise them a better future. If given absolute power, he said, he would assume total responsibility for the country. In the elections of 1930 and 1932, the Nazis became the largest and most powerful party in Germany.

Despite the many distinguished contributions that Jews had made to German society and culture over the centuries, Hitler's

propaganda described Jews as an inferior race and the origina-
tors of all that was hostile to Nazi goals, including Communism,
pacifism, internationalism, and even Christianity. The Jews, he
said, were a threat to Aryan racial purity and a source of "ideo-
logical infection."

Like his nationalism, Hitler's racial theories appealed strongly
to many Germans. After the elections of 1930, the thousand-
year-old German Jewish community (numbering about half a
million people) watched with fear and disbelief as the Nazis rose
in power. In January 1933, Hitler was appointed chancellor of
Germany. He soon demanded and was granted emergency pow-
ers for four years, after which he ruled by decree. He quickly
brought the republic to an end and established a totalitarian
regime. Hitler proceeded to outlaw all other political parties and
many institutions, including labor unions and youth and social
organizations. Churches, while not closed down, were harassed.
All communications media, including newspapers, radio, and
film, became operations of the state and were used to manipu-
late public opinion.

Although many Germans were upset by Hitler's rise in power
and his methods of rule, the majority supported him or remained
silent. He used force to achieve his ends, and the penalties for
those who did not support him included arrests, beatings,
imprisonment without trial, and torture by the dreaded Gestapo.
This silenced Hitler's opponents.

Hitler's anti-Jewish program was systematically implemented.
Jews were not permitted to teach in public schools or universities. They could not hold public office or civil service jobs
or work in the communications industry. They were eventually

prohibited from working in medicine, law, business, and most private employment. As they lost their means of livelihood, the Jews were segregated from their "Aryan" neighbors. Jewish children were not permitted to attend the same schools as non-Jewish children, and Jews were forbidden to marry or employ non-Jews. Many stores, shops, hotels, and restaurants would not serve Jews.

As Hitler's armies conquered more and more of Europe, it became increasingly difficult for Jews to leave. France eventually surrendered to Germany, and in June 1941 the German armies attacked the Soviet Union despite their nonaggression pact with Stalin.

The Nazis were ruthless. Captured partisans were tortured and killed in Gestapo prisons. Resistance, and especially the killing of soldiers or policemen by partisans, was avenged with the slaughter of hostages.

Hitler adopted the "Final Solution" to solve the Jewish question. The plan was to exterminate the Jews, and everywhere in conquered Europe he implemented this policy. Jews were systematically rounded up and transported like cattle in crowded, sealed freight trains to extermination camps. Some of these concentration camps, including Auschwitz and Treblinka, were in Poland. Others, such as Dachau, Buchenwald, and Bergen-Belsen, were in Germany.

Upon arrival, numbers were tattooed on all prisoners' arms. Since Leviticus 19:28 says that we should not tattoo our bodies, this was an added insult to the Jewish prisoners. The men and women were separated, most never to see their family members again.

Many prisoners were worked to death by criminals serving the SS. Others died as a result of the poor conditions in the camps. Some perished as a result of hideous medical experiments; even more were systematically gassed or shot and then either buried or burned in crematories. Guards with machine guns watched from towers; high voltage fences surrounded the compounds.

An estimated six million Jews were systematically murdered. In addition, millions of non-Jews in Poland, Czechoslovakia, Russia, and elsewhere became victims of the Nazis.

In February 1945, the SS abandoned Auschwitz, and in May World War II ended.

It is bad enough when a person is singled out for persecution and discrimination and experiences all forms of prejudice simply because he or she is a member of a particular group. But when six million members of your own group are murdered over a short period of years; when 40 to 50 percent of the entire world population of Jews is annihilated; and when parents and grandparents, children, aunts, uncles, cousins, and friends become victims of systematic slaughter, the concept of the Holocaust indeed becomes an overwhelmingly painful nightmare.

The more one thinks about the Holocaust, the more unbelievable, frightening, and horrifying it becomes. The reaction of the Jewish victims themselves was of disbelief and denial. The reaction of the governments of the world, even when evidence of the death camps was confirmed, was the same. More and more evidence shows that even before America's entry into the war, U.S. government officials were informed of the existence of extermination camps and other atrocities. As difficult as it is to believe, for political or other reasons, no official protests were made and no action was taken to intervene in this outrageous situation. The 1930s were a time of high unemployment and increased anti-Semitism in the United States (higher unemployment and a rise in anti-Semitism often seem to go hand in hand). Instead of immigration quotas being relaxed to accept more Jews fleeing the Nazis, they actually became more restrictive. Thus, the situation for the Jews of Europe was grim.

Isolated stories of heroic escapes, rescues, and survivals pale in contrast to the overall story of one of the most horrifying acts of terrorism ever perpetrated.

In a recent visit to a large San Francisco bookstore, I browsed through the section on Judaism. Three-quarters of the books on the shelves were devoted to the Holocaust. Alongside the Bible, the Talmud, and other books of Judaica were dozens of volumes on the history of the Holocaust and the personal memoirs of Holocaust survivors and witnesses.

Many universities now have Holocaust studies programs. Trips to Israel routinely include visits to monuments commemorating the Holocaust. The Holocaust Museum in Washington, D.C., is included on the "must-see" list of thousands of visitors to the capital. Official political tours to Germany and Eastern Europe often include visits to the sites of the death camps.

Jews recall the Holocaust during High Holiday religious services. It is mentioned at Passover when we remember the Exodus of the Jews from Egypt. It is recalled again on Holocaust Remembrance Day, Yom HaShoah, each spring. (There is also a day of remembrance called *Kristallnacht* on November 9—the date in 1938 when the Nazis began the systematic murder and destruction of German and European Jews and their homes, synagogues, and property.)

Jews around the world must never forget the atrocities and the systematic, cold-blooded attempt to annihilate their people. Yom HaShoah is commemorated in a number of ways by Jewish congregations. Very often there is a lighting of six candles, one for each million killed. A seventh candle may represent the non-Jews murdered in the Holocaust, or to honor those who aided Jews at the risk of their own lives.

In the face of the emergence of neo-Nazis and the rise of the movement to deny that the Holocaust ever took place, it is more important than ever for not only Jews, but the entire civilized world to say, "Never again."

A Call for Understanding
and Community

When we hear a person make a statement such as "It was the Christian thing to do" or "He's an upstanding Christian in the community," we tend to feel comfortable in knowing that the person being referred to is good, kind, upstanding, and understanding. This is generally the case.

The image of a churchgoing family man or woman has always implied qualities that we look up to, emulate, and seek in friends. I know from speaking to my Christian friends that they admire these same qualities and attributes in their Jewish colleagues who attend services, practice their religion, and maintain a firm belief in God.

There is an expression in Yiddish that has a similar connotation. To refer to a person of honor and dignity, a decent, admirable person of quality, people say, "He's a mensch"—a good human being.

I can admire a person who lives his or her life as a good Christian, because Jesus embodied those same qualities and so much more. He preached goodness, mercy, understanding, and love.

These are the traits still admired in our fellow human beings, regardless of race, religion, or nationality.

Because of the part the Jewish people have played in biblical history and their role as the Chosen People, many people are genuinely concerned for the salvation of the Jews. How can I not be aware that there are those who believe that because I have not accepted Jesus, I will not be "saved"?

I hope that my Christian friends, after reading this book, have a better understanding of Judaism and the Jewish belief system. I also hope they can accept that I, for one, am most concerned that we all work together to make our limited time on Earth one of sharing, understanding, tolerance, compassion, and community.

No matter what your concept is of an afterlife, salvation, or heaven and hell, our time spent here on earth will be better spent in an atmosphere of loving kindness and tolerance of one another. As my wife says, "We're all in the boat together."

I pray that we can all take to heart the words of both Hillel, "What is hateful to you, do not do to your neighbor," and Jesus, "In everything do to others as you would have them do to you" (Matthew 7:12).

Let us work together to help make this often-troubled world one of peace and harmony.

Shalom!

Glossary and Pronunciation Guide

Anote on pronunciation: The one sound in Hebrew and Yiddish that is not common in English is represented here as "ch." It often causes a problem for people not familiar with producing the sound, especially since it is considered "guttural." The easiest way to describe it is to mimic the sound of "Ach" in the German phrase, "Ach du lieber!" Carry this "Ach" sound over to the Hebrew word for bread, "challah" (pronounced: chah-lah), and you've got it. Good luck! (If you can't pronounce the "ch" sound, just use a softer "h" sound, as in "hah-lah." It works adequately, and people will understand you.)

When there are two pronunciations for the same word, the first is the Hebrew pronunciation, and the second is either the Yiddish or the more common pronunciation.

afikomen (AH-fee-KO-men). Greek for "dessert." The middle of the three pieces of matzo (unleavened bread) used at the Passover seder.

aliyah (ah-lee-YAH or ah-LEE-yah). Hebrew for "going up." The recitation of a special blessing before and after the reading of each Torah portion. Each section of the Torah portion is also called an *aliyah*. When one moves to Israel, it is called "making *aliyah*."

Amidah (ah-mee-DAH). Basic to the religious service, the Amidah consists of personal prayers and blessings; it is generally recited silently while standing.

Apocrypha (a-PAHK-r'-fah). A group of books not included in the final version of the Bible, but considered important; it includes the Books of Maccabees and the stories of Judith and Hannah.

Aramaic (air-uh-MAY-ik). A Semitic language (related to Hebrew) spoken in biblical times; it was the language of Jesus.

Ashkenazic (ahsh-ken-AH-zik). Refers to Jews who settled in Middle, Northern, and Eastern Europe; their language, food, and many religious and social customs differ from that of the Sephardic Jews.

avarot (ah-vah-ROTE). The willow (plural), mentioned in the Bible as "willows of the brook." One of the four species of plants used in the celebration of the holiday of Sukkot.

avelut (ah-vay-LOOT). Hebrew for "mourning." The mourning period for one's parents, starting from the day of the death and continuing for an entire Jewish calendar year.

BCE. Before the Common Era. This term is generally used by Jews instead of BC.

Ba'al Shem Tov (b'ahl-shem-tohv). The founder of modern Hasidism (born Israel ben Eliezer in 1698).

bar mitzvah (bahr MITZ-vah). Hebrew for "son of the commandment." The term used to indicate that a boy has reached "adulthood" in the Jewish religion. Generally observed at age thirteen, bar mitzvah is usually celebrated with a religious ceremony, and often a reception.

bat mitzvah (baht MITZ-vah). Also referred to as bas mitzvah (bahs MITZ-vah). Hebrew for "daughter of the commandment." The term used to indicate that a girl has reached "adulthood" in the Jewish religion. Generally observed at age thirteen, it is celebrated in the same manner as a bar mitzvah in Liberal congregations. (Bat mitzvah was originally celebrated at age twelve in recognition of a girl's earlier maturation, and this tradition is still followed in many Orthodox and other congregations.)

beitzah (bay-TZAH). The roasted hard-boiled egg on the seder plate at Passover, which commemorates the festival sacrifice brought to the temple during the spring; it also reminds us of the destruction of the temples in Jerusalem.

Bible. The Hebrew Bible includes three sections: (1) the Pentateuch (or Five Books of Moses)—Genesis, Exodus, Leviticus, Numbers, and Deuteronomy; (2) the Prophets—the books of Joshua, Judges, Samuel I and II, Kings I and II, Isaiah, Jeremiah, Ezekiel, and the twelve "minor" prophets (Hosea, Joel, Amos, Obadiah, Jonah, Micah, Nahum, Habakkuk, Zephaniah, Haggai, Zechariah, Malachi), which count as one book; and (3) the holy Writings (Psalms, Proverbs, Job, Song of Songs, Ruth, Lamentations, Ecclesiastes, Esther, Daniel, Ezra and Nehemiah, and Chronicles I and II).

bimah (bee-MAH, or BEE-mah). The raised platform in the front of the synagogue sanctuary from which religious services are led.

b'nai mitzvah (b-NAY mitz-VAH). Hebrew for "children of the commandment" (*b'nai* is the plural of bar and bat.) A situation in which more than one child is celebrating a bar and/or bat mitzvah at the same time.

brit; brit milah; bris (breet, brit mee-LAH, bris). In Hebrew, *brit* means "covenant," and *milah* means "circumcision." These terms generally refer to the ceremony and act marking the covenant of circumcision.

brit habat (breet, or brit ha-BAHT). Hebrew for "covenant of the daughter." Generally used to refer to the naming of a baby girl, often at a synagogue service.

cantor. The person who leads the congregation in those portions of prayer that are sung. Trained in liturgical music, the cantor, along with the rabbi, leads the synagogue service; the cantor is often a teacher as well.

CE Common Era. This term is generally used by Jews instead of AD, or *Anno Domini,* which is Latin for "in the year of our Lord."

chai (chy). This word means "life" and is part of the phrase "L'Chaim!" The two letters making up this Hebrew word have a numerical equivalent of eighteen, which has a special significance to Jews. Modern Jews often make financial gifts to charities in multiples of eighteen.

challah (chah-lah). The traditional braided egg bread, used on Shabbat and holidays.

cheder (CHAY-der). A religious school.

cholent (CHO-lent—this is an exception to the rule, and pronounced with the normal English "ch" sound, as in the English word *chose*). A special type of stew generally containing beef, barley, beans, and potatoes. It is kept warm on the stove over a very low flame throughout the Sabbath, since lighting a new flame for cooking is forbidden on Shabbat in the homes of observant Jews.

chuppah (choo-PAH or CHOO-pah). The wedding canopy; it may be an embroidered cloth or a *tallit* (prayer shawl), and is a symbol of the groom's home, which the bride is entering. It may also be thought of as a symbol of the tents of the ancient Hebrews.

chutzpah (CHUHTZ-puh). Yiddish word for nerve, guts, gall, or arrogance.

Conservative. One of the several major Jewish religious movements, developed in the United States in the twentieth century; Conservative Judaism represents a mix of both traditional and more modern views, accommodating the needs of Jewish life in modern society while also accepting the divine inspiration of the law of the Torah.

daven (DAH-vin). Yiddish word for the phrase "to pray."

Diaspora (dy-AS-puh-ruh). Anyplace outside the land of Israel where Jewish people have lived. The vast majority of the Jewish population has lived outside Israel throughout most of its history.

dreidel (DRAY-del). A four-sided top used in a traditional game played at Hanukkah time. The letters on the dreidel symbolize the words, "A great miracle happened there" (in Israel, "A great miracle happened *here*").

erev (EH-rev). The word means "the evening of" and is usually used with the name of a holiday, such as "Erev Shabbat," the eve of Sabbath, the time at which the holiday actually begins.

etrog (EH-trahg). The citron fruit, mentioned in the Bible as "the fruit of goodly trees." One of the four species of plants used in the celebration of the holiday of Sukkot.

gelt (gehlt). Yiddish for money.

Gemara (geh-MAH-rah). Aramaic for "study." Written commentaries, discussions, and deductions interspersed into each paragraph or section of the Mishnah, which give insight into historical, spiritual, ethical, and legal issues. The combination of the Mishnah plus the Gemara is called the Talmud.

gemilut hasadim (geh-mee-LOOT chah-sah-DEEM). As described in the Talmud, this term defines acts of goodwill, including visiting the ill, providing clothing for the needy, giving comfort to mourners, accompanying the dead to their graves, being hospitable to strangers, and giving assistance to brides.

get (gett). A Jewish divorce document that indicates a religious divorce; this is completely separate from civil divorce proceedings. Although most divorced Jewish couples do not apply for a religious divorce, more observant or Orthodox Jews view it as essential.

gonif (GAH-nif). The Yiddish word for "thief," often used to describe a somewhat dishonest merchant or an untrustworthy or shady character.

hadassim (chah-dah-SEEM). The branch of the myrtle, mentioned in the Bible as "boughs of leafy trees." One of the four species of plants used in the celebration of the holiday of Sukkot.

haftarah (hahf-ta-RAH or hahf-TOH-rah). A portion from one of the books of the Prophets read during religious services; it often reflects the content of the Torah reading and was instituted at a time in history when reading from the actual Torah was forbidden under penalty of death.

Haggadah (hah-gah-DAH or hah-GAH-dah). The booklet read during the Passover seder that contains prayers, songs, and psalms and recounts the story of the Exodus of the Jewish People.

Halachah (hah-lah-CHAH). A term that describes the entire body of Jewish law.

hamantaschen (HUM-en-tahsh-en). Little triangular-shaped pastries filled with fruit, cheese, or poppy seeds; popular during the festival of Purim.

hametz (CHUM-etz). Any food product that is leavened, fermented, or is likely to ferment, any of which would make it "not kosher" for the Passover holiday; included are bread, cakes, cookies, beer, liquor, and many types of cereals.

Hanukkah (chah-noo-KAH or CHAH-nuh-kah). The winter holiday commemorating the victory of the Maccabees over the Syrian Seleucids and the rededication of the temple in Jerusalem (164 BCE). As part of this rededication, a miracle occurred wherein the holy oil—enough to kindle the temple light for only one day—burned for eight days.

hanukkiah (chah-noo-kee-YAH or CHAH-noo-KEE-yah). The Hanukkah candelabra, also known as a menorah; it contains nine branches or sections, one for each of the eight days of Hanukkah, and a ninth, the *shammes* ("servant" or "helper") candle.

haroset (chah-RO-set). A special mixture of nuts, fruits, cinnamon, and wine (or juice), used in the Passover seder; symbolic of the bricks and mortar used by the Jewish slaves in performing hard labor.

Hashem (hah-SHEM). One of several names used to refer to God; it means "the name" in Hebrew.

Hasid (CHAH-seed). A member of the Hasidic movement.

Hasidism (CHAH-SEE-diz'm). The ultra-Orthodox movement founded by Ba'al Shem Tov during the eighteenth century and based on pious spiritualism and Jewish mysticism in the form of the Kabbalah.

havdalah (hahv-dah-LAH or hahv-DAH-lah). Hebrew for "separation." The evening service and ceremony marking the end of the Sabbath or other holidays; three special symbols are used in the ceremony—a goblet of wine, a container of sweet-smelling spices, and a braided, multiwicked candle.

havurah (chah-voo-RAH). A group that acts as an "extended family" with whom to celebrate holidays, give support in times of crisis, enjoy religious and nonreligious events, and share a religious commonality.

hazzan (chah-ZAHN). Hebrew for "cantor" (masculine).

hazzanit (chah-zahn-EET). Hebrew for "cantor" (feminine).

heksher (HEK-shuhr). A special symbol indicating that a product is kosher and has been prepared under rabbinic supervision.

Holocaust. The attempt by Adolf Hitler and the Nazis to systematically exterminate the Jewish people, resulting in the death of six million Jews.

Holocaust Remembrance Day. Yom HaShoah in Hebrew, the day set aside to remember victims of the Holocaust.

Israel Independence Day. Yom HaAtzma'ut in Hebrew; marks the anniversary of the May 15, 1948, founding of the state of Israel.

Kabbalah (kah-bah-LAH or kah-BAH-lah). Jewish mysticism, based on the *Zohar* and other writings.

Kaddish (KAH-dish). The mourner's prayer. Although having nothing to do with death, it indicates faith, distress, and submission to the will of God. (Not to be confused with Kiddush.)

karpas (KAHR-pahs). Parsley, potato, or another vegetable used as part of the Passover seder; the *karpas* is dipped in salted water and eaten as a reminder of tears we shed as slaves before the Exodus.

kashrut (kahsh-root). The dietary rules and restrictions as set down in the Bible and elaborated on by the Rabbis; it includes particulars regarding the ritual slaughter of animals, the separation of dairy and meat, and so on.

ketubbah (keh-too-BAH or keh-TOO-bah). The Jewish marriage decree; it is written in Aramaic and may be decorated with designs, paintings, drawings, and calligraphy.

kibbutz (kee-BOOTZ). An Israeli agricultural cooperative or collective farm; many *kibbutzim* (plural) now include manufacturing and tourism.

kibitz (KIH-bitz). A Yiddish word generally referring to endless commentary, joking, needling, second-guessing, criticizing, and teasing; a *kibitzer* is someone who's always talking to you, telling you jokes and stories, or commenting while you're trying to work, play your hand at cards, or pay attention to something else.

Kiddush (kih-DOOSH or KIH-duhsh). The blessing said over wine ("The fruit of the vine") on Shabbat and on holidays. (Not to be confused with Kaddish.)

kippah (kee-pah). A cap or skullcap customarily worn to symbolize reverence and submission to God. It may be worn always or only during prayer or religious study; traditionally the kippah was worn only by men, but today it is worn by many women as well. In Yiddish, the word used is *yarmulke* (YAHR-mool-kah), for "cap."

kittel (KIT-tl). A white robe. It is worn by some men during High Holy Day religious services and by the bridegroom on his wedding day. It also serves as a burial shroud.

Kohen (KO-hayn). A person directly descended from Aaron, the brother of Moses, all of whose descendants were priests in early Judaic history; today, *Kohanim* (plural: ko-hay-NEEM) perform certain religious rituals in Orthodox and many Conservative congregations.

Kol Nidre (kohl NEE-dray). The special evening service and prayer opening the Yom Kippur holiday; chanted to a haunting melody just before sunset, this prayer releases one from promises or vows made to God that cannot be fulfilled.

kosher (KOH-shur). The term used to describe foods that comply with the biblical and rabbinical dietary rules and restrictions.

L'Chaim (luh-CHY-um). [Rhymes with "tuh-TRY-um"] Yiddish toast that means, "To Life!"

Ladino (lah-DEE-noh). Spoken by the early Mediterranean Jews known as Sephardim, this language is a combination of Hebrew, Spanish, and Portuguese.

latkes (LAHT-kehs). Potato pancakes; one of the traditional holiday foods eaten at Hanukkah.

lulav (LOO-lahv). The date palm. One of the four species of plants used in the celebration of the holiday of Sukkot.

Maimonides, Moses. Rabbi Moshe Ben Maimon (1135–1204), a great Jewish rabbi, writer, scholar, and philosopher; he wrote the *Mishnah Torah* and *The Guide for the Perplexed.*

maror (mah-rohr). Bitter herbs, a part of the Passover ceremony; they symbolize the bitterness of the slavery the Jews experienced in Egypt before the Exodus.

matzo (MAH-tzah). The flat, unleavened bread eaten during the Passover holiday; it is often referred to as "the bread of affliction." (Also matzah, matzoh.)

maven (MAY-v'n). The Yiddish word to describe a so-called expert, as in the personalized license plate: TAXMAVEN.

mazel tov (MAH-z'l tohv). Hebrew for "good luck." A common expression for "congratulations."

megillah (m'gee-LAH or m'GIH-lah). The scroll on which the Book of Esther is written and from which the story of Purim is read; the word means "scroll" and is the origin of the expression "the whole megillah."

menorah (meh-NAW-rah). The Hanukkah candelabra (see *hanukkiah*).

mensch (mensh). A Yiddish word used to describe someone of honor, dignity; a decent, admirable person of quality.

mezuzah (m'zoo-ZAH or meh-ZUH-zah). A small container fastened to the doorpost of a house within which is a scroll containing two paragraphs from Deuteronomy as well as three Hebrew letters that spell one of God's names.

Midrash (mid-RAHSH or MID-rahsh). Hebrew for "investigation." A collection of rabbinical questions, stories, and commentaries on the Bible.

mikvah (mik-VAH, or MIK-vah). The ritual bath visited by observant Jews for religious and spiritual immersion in preparation for Shabbat, or for women as part of their regular monthly cycle; also used as part of the religious conversion ritual.

minyan (meen-YAHN or MIN-yun). A quorum of ten adults, the minimum number required to form a congregation for prayer purposes; an Orthodox service requires ten men.

Mishnah (meesh-NAH, or MISH-nuh). Hebrew for "recapitulation." Written by the earliest "rabbinic" scholars, the Mishnah is based on the oral law and provides explanations and amplifications of temple rituals, holidays, family life and observances, and agricultural issues, as well as proverbs and philosophical observations.

mitzvah (meetz-VAH or MITZ-vah). Hebrew for "commandment." "Bar mitzvah" or "bat mitzvah" means "son" or "daughter of the commandment." In common usage, it means a "good deed" or a kind, considerate act.

mohel (MO-hel, or moil). A specialist trained and highly experienced in performing the ritual circumcision procedure.

motzi (MO-tzee) or **HaMotzi.** A prayer before meals that gives thanks for the "bread of the earth," bread being symbolic of food in general.

Oneg Shabbat (o-nayg shah-BAHT). An informal gathering held after a Shabbat service.

Orthodox. Of the several major Jewish religious movements, Orthodox Judaism is the most traditional, believing that the Law of God was given to Moses on Mount Sinai, and that the Torah, therefore, is divine.

pareve (pahrv or PAHR-veh). A "neutral" food group; it includes all fish having fins and scales and all foods that grow in the earth (fruits, vegetables, grains, fungi, seeds, nuts, etc.). The rules governing kosher foods permit the eating of *pareve* foods with meat or dairy products.

Passover. The holiday celebrating the Exodus of the Jewish People from Egypt and their freedom from slavery. In Hebrew, the holiday is called *Pesach* (PAY-sahch)

Pentateuch. The Torah, encompassing the Five Books of Moses ("five scrolls" in Greek).

Pharisees. A group that lived in the Holy Land at the time of the Second Temple and around the time of Jesus; some consider these spiritual leaders and interpreters of the Torah to be the first rabbis.

pidyon haben (peed-YOHN hah-BEN). The "Redemption of the firstborn son" from a *Kohen* (Jewish priest); a ritual connected to the last of the ten plagues. The firstborn sons of the Jews were spared by God and therefore were considered as belonging to God.

Purim (POO-reem). The festival celebrating the story told in the Book of Esther (this book is written on a scroll called a *megillah)* wherein the Jews are saved from destruction.

rabbi. A rabbi is a seminary-trained and ordained member of the clergy who leads religious services, officiates at activities such as weddings and funerals, and teaches classes through the synagogue; the rabbi is the spiritual leader of a synagogue.

Reconstructionism. A religious movement whose concept is that Judaism is a "civilization" that evolves and progresses and must therefore be rediscovered and reinterpreted on an ongoing basis; founded by Rabbi Mordecai Kaplan in the twentieth century.

Reform. One of the several major Jewish religious movements, Reform Judaism is a combination of traditional practice and modification of that practice, emphasizing egalitarianism and a need to interpret the Jewish tradition from a modern and individual perspective.

Rosh Hashanah (roash hah-shah-nah). The Jewish New Year; along with Yom Kippur, it is one of the High Holidays, and is marked by the blowing of the shofar.

Rosh Hodesh (roash CHO-desh). The first day of every Jewish (lunar) month; considered a women's holiday.

sabra (SAHB-rah). A native-born Israeli.

sandek (SAHN-dek). The person who holds the baby during the religious circumcision ritual; may also be the godparent.

schlemiel (shleh-MEEL). A Yiddish term that describes a naive, simple, clumsy, gullible, and/or foolish person (usually a man).

schmaltz (shmahltz). A Yiddish word for rendered or melted chicken fat, used in cooking; also a slang word to describe something "corny."

schmendrick (SHMEN-drik). A Yiddish term that describes an unsuccessful, weak, unimpressive, and/or untrustworthy person (usually a man).

schnorrer (SHNUHR-er or SHNAWR-er). The Yiddish word that describes a beggar, bum, cheapskate, chiseler, moocher, or panhandler.

seder (SAY-der). Hebrew for "order." Generally refers to the Passover service and meal.

Sephardic (seh-FAHR-dik). Refers to Jews who settled in Spain, Portugal, and other Mediterranean regions; their language, culture, food, and many religious and social customs differ from those of the Ashkenazic Jews.

Shabbat (shah-BAHT). Hebrew for "Sabbath." The Yiddish word for Sabbath, also commonly used, is *Shabbos* (SHAH-bus).

shalom (shah-LOAM). The Hebrew word meaning "peace," "hello," and "good-bye"; it is a common greeting (and an important word to know).

shammes (shah-MAHSH). The "servant" or "helper" candle in the *hanukkiah* (menorah); it is an "extra" (ninth) candle used to light the others.

Shavuot (shah-voo-OAT or shah-VOO-oat). Hebrew for "weeks"; it is the holiday celebrating the harvest; it falls in the late spring, seven weeks after Passover, and also commemorates the deliverance of the Ten Commandments on Mount Sinai.

Shechinah (sheh-CHEE-nah). The Hebrew word that describes God's divine presence. It is used by many today to refer to God's feminine attributes or the "female side" of God.

Shema (sheh-MAH). The passage most common to Jewish prayer and religious services; it is from Deuteronomy 6:4, and declares, "Hear, O Israel: The LORD is our God, the LORD is one." "The Eternal" is substituted for "The Lord" in translations desiring gender-neutrality.

Sheva Brachot (SHEH-vah b'rah-CHOAT). The seven special blessings recited during the marriage ceremony.

shiksa (SHIK-suh). Yiddish for a non-Jewish woman; generally used to describe a young woman. It can be used in an affectionate/friendly, neutral, or negative manner.

shiva (SHIH-vah). Hebrew for "seven." The mourning period; it begins on the day of the funeral and lasts for seven days. A family is said to be "sitting shivah" during this period and receives friends and relatives paying condolence calls.

Shoah (sho-AH). Hebrew for "Holocaust," as in Yom HaShoah, Holocaust Remembrance Day.

shochet (SHOH-chet or SHAH-chet). A person specially trained in the ritual slaughter of animals in order that the meat be considered kosher.

shofar (sho-FAHR). A wind instrument made from a ram's horn; the blowing of the shofar is heard on the Jewish High Holidays—Rosh Hashanah and Yom Kippur.

shtetl (SHTEH-tl). A small town; used to describe those towns once inhabited by Ashkenazic Jews in Eastern Europe.

shtick. Yiddish for a "piece," as in a piece of comedy material; a routine, gesture, characterization, or device.

shul (shool). A German/Yiddish word meaning "school"; can also refer to a synagogue.

siddur (see-DOOHR). A prayer book.

simcha (SEEM-chah). A joyous occasion; a celebration or party.

Simchat Torah (seem-chat toh-RAH or TOH-rah). The celebration marking the day we complete the reading of Deuteronomy, the last of the Five Books of Moses, and immediately begin the Torah-reading cycle again with the first book, Genesis; the occasion is a time for singing, dancing with the Torah, and other expressions of great joy.

siman tov (SEE-mahn tohv). Hebrew for "Good omen"; an expression for "congratulations."

sofer (SO-fehr). A scribe who is specially trained in the writing of the Torah scrolls and other religious documents.

sukkah (soo-KAH or SUH-kah). The structure erected for the holiday of Sukkot. The stars should be visible through the roof of the booth or hut; from the walls and roof are hung leaves, gourds, fruits, and other symbols of the harvest.

Sukkot (soo-KOAT). The fall festival celebrating the harvest and commemorating the forty years the Israelites wandered in the desert, living in portable dwellings, waiting to enter the Promised Land.

tallit (tah-LEET). A prayer shawl containing special fringes (*tzitzit*) at each of the four corners; God said to Moses, "Speak to the Children of Israel and bid them to affix fringes to the corners of the garments" so that whenever these fringes are seen, they will be reminded of God's commandments. (Tallis [TAH-liss] in Yiddish.)

Talmud (TAHL-mood). The Talmud, which is made up of the Mishnah and the Gemara, was completed about 500 CE and is like an encyclopedia of Jewish law, life, and thought; it is filled with spiritual wisdom, humor, advice, anecdotes, and rabbinical arguments and puzzles.

Tanakh (tah-NAHCH). The Hebrew word for Bible. It is an acronym, made up of the first letters of the words *Torah* (the Five Books of Moses), *Nevi'im* (Prophets), and *Ketuvim* (Writings).

tashlich (tahsh-LEECH). Hebrew for "casting off." The prophet Micah (7:19) said: "You will cast all our sins into the depths of the sea"; it is a centuries-old ritual where, on the afternoon of Rosh Hashanah (the Jewish New Year), people meet and toss their sins (symbolized by bread crumbs) into a body of water.

tefillin (teh-FILL-in). Used as part of traditional prayer ritual, tefillin (also known as phylacteries) are small boxes containing parchment on which are written verses from the books of Exodus and Deuteronomy. Attached to the boxes are leather straps used to fasten them to the left arm (right arm if left-handed) and forehead during prayer.

Temples, the First and Second. Built in Jerusalem by King Solomon around 950 BCE, the First Temple was a marvelous religious structure containing a central room known as the Holy of Holies, which housed the sacred Ark of the Covenant. The First Temple was destroyed by the Babylonians in 586 BCE, but was restored around 516 BCE; it was rebuilt on a grand scale by Herod around 30 BCE, but the Second Temple was destroyed by the Romans in 70 CE.

tikkun olam (tee-KOON oh-LAHM). Hebrew for the act of "repairing the world," including the performing of *mitzvot* and following the Ten Commandments, as well as social acts such as working for peace, the environment, and an end to bigotry and injustice.

Tisha B'Av (tee-SHAH buh-AHV or TISH-ah buh-AHV). Also called the Day of Lamentation, this holiday commemorates the destruction of the First and Second Temples in Jerusalem as well as other events destructive to the Jewish people; the day is marked by fasting and observing other traditional Jewish signs of mourning. In the synagogue, the Book of Lamentations is read.

Torah (toh-RAH or TOH-rah). The scroll containing the Five Books of Moses (Pentateuch): Genesis, Exodus, Leviticus, Numbers, and Deuteronomy; the term "to study Torah" also refers to Jewish learning and study in general.

treif (trayf). Hebrew for "torn to pieces." Any animal or food not slaughtered or prepared according to Jewish ritual laws, that is unfit for consumption or does not fall into the food categories considered "permissible" by the Torah.

Tu B'Shevat (too bish-VAHT). The Jewish Arbor Day; this "New Year of the Trees" is celebrated by planting seeds and trees, eating fruit, and recognizing the importance of nature and ecology.

tzedakah (tzuh-dah-KAH or tzeh-DAH-kah). Charitable donations; the concept of giving in a cheerful and generous (righteous) manner.

ulpan (ool-PAHN). An intensive Hebrew language course; a school, generally in Israel, where conversational Hebrew is taught.

Yahrzeit (YAHR-tzite). The anniversary of a death, generally marked by prayer and the lighting of a special candle that burns an entire day; the Yahrzeit candle may also be lighted on the eve of Yom Kippur and at the end of other festivals such as Passover, *Shavuot*, and Sukkot.

yarmulke (YAHR-mool-kah). Yiddish for the skullcap that is worn to symbolize man's reverence and submission to God. It may be worn all the time or only during prayer and study (*kippah* in Hebrew).

yenta (YEN-teh). A Yiddish word used to describe a gossip or rumormonger; a tactless person (generally a woman, but not always).

yeshiva (yeh-shee-VAH or yeh-SHEE-vah). A Jewish religious academy, school, college, or university.

Yiddish (YIH-dish). The language spoken by the Jews of Germany and Eastern Europe (the Ashkenazim); a combination of Hebrew and German, with other words from various regions thrown in.

Yom HaShoah (yohm-hah-sho-AH). Holocaust Remembrance Day; it falls in the spring, about two weeks after the Passover holiday, and recalls the victims of the Holocaust.

Yom Kippur (yohm kee-POOR, or yohm KIH-purr). The Day of Atonement; the holiest and most solemn day of the year, the day on which one's fate during the coming year is determined.

zeroah (zeh-ROH-ah). At Passover, the shank bone of a lamb on the seder plate; symbolic of the Paschal (Passover) sacrifice offered at the temple in Jerusalem in early times.

Zohar (ZOH-hahr). A book of Jewish mysticism and commentary on the Torah "discovered" at the end of the thirteenth century; it claims that hidden spiritual messages and the secrets of creation could be found by carefully examining the biblical text, although its authenticity is challenged by some scholars.

Recommended Reading

Ariel, David S. *What Do Jews Believe? The Spiritual Foundations of Judaism.* New York: Schocken Books, 1996.

Blech, Benjamin. *The Complete Idiot's Guide to Jewish History and Culture.* New York: Alpha Books, 1999.

———. *The Complete Idiot's Guide to Understanding Judaism.* New York: Alpha Books, 1999.

Cox, Harvey. *Common Prayers: Faith, Family, and a Christian's Journey through the Jewish Year.* Boston: Houghton Mifflin Company, 2001.

Diamant, Anita, and Howard Cooper. *Living a Jewish Life: A Guide for Starting, Learning, Celebrating, and Parenting.* New York: HarperCollins Publishers, 1991.

Dosick, Wayne D. *Living Judaism: The Complete Guide to Jewish Belief, Tradition, and Practice.* New York: Harper San Francisco, 1998.

Einstein, Stephen J., and Lydia Kukoff. *Every Person's Guide to Judaism.* New York: Union of American Hebrew Congregations Press, 1989.

Einstein, Stephen J. (comp.), et al. *Introduction to Judaism—A Source Book.* New York: Union of American Hebrew Congregations Press, 1999.

Eisenberg, Robert. *Boychiks in the Hood.* New York: HarperCollins Publishers, 1995.

Fisher, Eugene J., ed. *The Jewish Roots of Christian Liturgy.* New Jersey: Paulist Press, 1990.

Frank, Anne. *The Diary of a Young Girl.* New York: Random House, 1997.

Frymer-Kensky, Tikva, David Novak, Peter Ochs, David Fox Sandmel, and Michael A. Signer. *Christianity in Jewish Terms.* Colorado: Westview Press, 2000.

Himelstein, Rabbi Shmuel. *The Jewish Primer: Questions and Answers on Jewish Faith and Culture.* New York: Facts on File, 1990.

Kertzer, Rabbi Morris N., and Rabbi Lawrence A. Hoffman. *What Is a Jew?* New York: Collier Books, 1997.

Kolatch, Alfred J. *The Jewish Book of Why.* Vol. 1 and 2. New York: Jonathan David Publishers, 1987.

Kushner, Harold S. *To Life! A Celebration of Jewish Being and Thinking.* New York: Warner Books, 1994.

Neusner, Jacob. *An Introduction to Judaism: A Textbook and Reader.* Louisville: Westminster John Knox Press, 1992.

Rosenberg, Roy A. *The Concise Guide to Judaism: History, Practice, Faith.* New York: Meridian Books, 1994.

Rosten, Leo. *The Joys of Yiddish.* New York: Pocket Books/McGraw-Hill, 1999.

Starr-Glass, David. *Simple Guide to Judaism.* Baltimore: Paul Norbury, 1997.

Steinberg, Milton. *Basic Judaism.* New York: Harcourt Brace, 1986.

Vermes, Geza. *The Religion of Jesus the Jew.* Minneapolis: Fortress Press, 1993.

Wouk, Herman. *The Will to Live On—This Is Our Heritage.* New York: Cliff Street Books, 2001.

Wouk, Herman. *This is My God: The Jewish Way of Life.* New York: Little, Brown, 1992.

Index